WALK OFF
Weight
JOURNAL

The information in this book is meant to supplement, not replace, proper exercise training. All forms of exercise pose some inherent risks. The editors and publisher advise readers to take full responsibility for their safety and know their limits. Before practicing the exercises in this book, be sure that your equipment is well-maintained, and do not take risks beyond your level of experience, aptitude, training, and fitness. The exercise and dietary programs in this book are not intended as a substitute for any exercise routine or dietary regimen that may have been prescribed by your doctor. As with all exercise and dietary programs, you should get your doctor's approval before beginning.

Mention of specific companies, organizations, or authorities in this book does not imply endorsement by the author or publisher, nor does mention of specific companies, organizations, or authorities imply their endorsement of this book, its author, or the publisher.

Internet addresses and telephone numbers given in this book were accurate at the time it went to press.

Printed in the United States of America
Rodale Inc. makes every effort to use acid-free ∞, recycled paper ♻.

Book design by Alyson Cameron

Library of Congress Cataloging-in-Publication Data
Stanten, Michele.
    Walk off weight journal : your daily push to permanent weight loss 3X as fast! / Michele Stanten.
        p.   cm.
    ISBN-13   978-1-60529-355-4   paperback
    ISBN-10   1-60529-355-5   paperback
  1. Walking.   2. Reducing exercises.   3. Physical fitness.   I. Title.
    RA781.65.S73 2010
    613.7'176—dc22

                                      2010000910

Distributed to the trade by Macmillan
2   4   6   8   10 9 7 5 3   paperback

We inspire and enable people to improve their lives and the world around them
For more of our products visit **rodalestore.com** or call 800-848-4735

WALK OFF
Weight
JOURNAL

YOUR DAILY PUSH TO PERMANENT WEIGHT LOSS 3X AS FAST!

BY MICHELE STANTEN, FITNESS DIRECTOR, **Prevention** ®

RODALE

INTRODUCTION

WHEN IT COMES TO starting a new diet and exercise program, no tool has more power to impact your long-term habits than keeping a journal. In one study, dieters who regularly recorded what they ate and when they exercised lost nearly twice as much weight as those who didn't keep track—of the 1,600 people (average age 55) in four cities across the United States, those who kept a journal 7 days a week lost an average of 18 pounds over 6 months, while those who didn't keep a record lost only 9.

Take it from Kathy Ashenfelter, the Walk Off Weight test panel's biggest loser, who dropped 22½ pounds and 12¾ inches in 8 weeks: "When I'd start to crave something, I'd look at my food log and see that I'd already eaten enough," she said. "Then I could resist the craving and move on." Seeing her meals in print helped Kathy distinguish between true hunger, when her body physically needed food—and fake hunger—when something else such as boredom or stress was driving her desire to eat.

Because of its ability to shed light on the daily habits that can hold you back, the *Walk Off Weight Journal* is the ideal companion to help you achieve your weight loss goals. Along with being a daily and weekly reminder writing it all down dramatically raises your awareness and helps you see the "big picture" of your relationship with exercise and food. You'll not only learn how much you eat and work out but also why, when, and how. This will enable you to discover patterns you weren't aware of—patterns that may be sabotaging your success. And until you know about and understand them, they're nearly impossible to change.

But don't worry—the main goal of keeping this journal isn't to police yourself: It's to learn about yourself. At the end of each week, you'll be able to look back and see how you succeeded—and where you need to keep trying. After a few weeks, you'll realize how the everyday choices you make can help you step closer to your food and fitness goals.

In the meantime, grab your sneaks, stock your pantry, and sharpen your pencils: It's time to start walking off weight!

—Michele Stanten, Fitness Director, Prevention.

HOW TO USE THIS JOURNAL

WALKING IS THE NUMBER ONE ACTIVITY of successful losers, but no one should have to go it alone. Let this journal be your guide for the next 4 months as you track your diet and follow the innovative Walk Off Weight (WOW) program.

The journal is easy to use! At the beginning of each week, you'll see a reminder list of all the walks and workouts you need to do during the next 7 days.

Each day, record your exercise in the Workout Log and note how it went. Remember to write down which routines you do each day, the time you start your workout, and how long you exercise, including warm-up and cool-down. Finally, at the end of the day, tally up how much you exercised. This is also a good time to plan for when you'll fit in your next day's workouts. Don't forget to rate your energy and self-confidence levels for the day, too. Reviewing your answers periodically can help you overcome obstacles and remind you of just how far you've come.

On the Food Log, write down the foods you eat and your portion sizes. This record will also help you make sure you are getting proper nutrition—enough fiber, calcium, fats, and protein to keep your engine running, and especially enough water and green tea, which you can read more about in chapter 7 of *Walk Off Weight*. If you're following our menu plan, rest easy knowing we've selected the right meals to help you meet your daily targets. Use the Daily Nutrition Goals row to check off the number of servings of each food group you consume throughout the day: grains and starches, dairy products, lean proteins, fruits, vegetables, and healthy fats. These details will ensure that you are getting the daily recommended doses of essential vitamins and minerals.

At the end of each week, use the Weekly Measurements Log to track your progress. All you need are a bathroom scale and a measuring tape. Try to weigh and measure yourself around the same time on the same scale each week. For the most accurate results, ask someone else to help with the measuring tape. There are also two places to rate your average energy and self-confidence, each day and for the week.

Starting at the bottom of the Weekly Measurements Log page, you'll find blank lines so you can add any other thoughts or observations about your week, including benefits or improvements you're noticing (such as sleeping better, not getting winded when climbing stairs) or whether you've had some difficulties following the plan.

Remember, the Walk Off Weight plan is a fitness guide, not a set-in-stone schedule. You can adjust the routines to make them easier or more challenging and move workouts around during the week to fit everything into your busy lifestyle.

Here are some sample daily journal pages to help you get the right idea:

WEEK 2 DAY 5   DATE *April 5, 2009*

WORKOUT LOG

WORKOUTS	TIME	DURATION
Basic Interval I	6:30 a.m.	30 min
Lower-Body Strength Workout	8:00 p.m.	30 min
	DAILY TOTAL EXERCISE TIME	1 hour

WORKOUT NOTES

How did you feel before? *I was pretty tired when I got up this morning, but once I started walking I felt energized!*

How did you feel after? *That was better than a cup of coffee!*

Any obstacles? *I had to review the exercises for the lower body workout several times until I got it, so it took me longer than expected*

Major accomplishment? *I did all the "make it harder" versions of the exercises in the Lower Body Strength Workout!*

Other notes: *Eating according to the guidelines today was tricky, but I'm surprised how much better I feel. I can't wait to see what I feel like this time next week!*

PERSONAL NOTES

ENERGY LEVEL (circle one)
1 being "I'm so tired I can't get out of bed" and **10 being** "I could dance all night!"

| 1 | 2 | 3 | 4 | 5 | ⑥ | 7 | 8 | 9 | 10 |

SELF-ESTEEM/SELF-CONFIDENCE (circle one)
1 being "I can't do anything right" and **10 being** "I'm ready to change the world!"

| 1 | 2 | 3 | 4 | 5 | 6 | 7 | ⑧ | 9 | 10 |

WEEK **2** DAY **5**

FOOD LOG

	FOOD/DRINKS	TIME	CALORIES
Breakfast	2 wholegrain waffles, 1 tbsp powdered sugar, 1/2 oz chopped walnuts, 3/4 cup strawberry halves, 1 cup green tea + 1 glass water before breakfast	9:00 a.m.	345
Lunch	1 egg made into egg salad with 2 tsp light mayo on 2 slices whole grain toast, 1 large orange, 1/2 cucumber, sliced, 1 tbsp light ranch dressing; 1 cup skim milk	1:00 p.m.	450
Snack	6 oz nonfat vanilla yogurt, 1/2 cup blueberries, 1 cup green tea + 2 glasses of water in the afternoon	3:30 p.m.	197
Dinner	4 oz Haddock, sauteed in 2 tsp olive oil, 1 cup steamed carrots, 3/4 cup brown rice, 1 cup skim milk	7:45 p.m.	550
Optional Snack	3 cups light microwave popcorn drizzled with 1 tbsp peanut butter, + 2 glasses of water in the evening	9:00 p.m.	172
		DAILY CALORIE TOTAL	1,714

DAILY NUTRITION GOALS:	Grains/Starches	Fruits	Vegetables	Dairy	Healthy Fats	Lean Proteins
	☒☒☒☒☒☒	☒☒☒	☒☒☒☐☐	☒☒☒	☒☒☒☐	☒☒☒
	Water	Green Tea	Optional (amount per day)			
	☒☒☒☒☒	☒☒☐	Fiber _30_ g Calcium 1,186 mg Vitamin D 298 IU			

BONUS TRACKER (*Record your blood sugar, track your medications, gauge your hunger, or make other notes here.*)

I got 7 hours of sleep last night.
I was only going to have 1 snack today, but the popcorn after dinner helped me go to bed without feeling hungry

Here are some sample weekly journal pages to help you get the right idea:

➤ DATE/TIME _04/7/09   8:30 a.m._

WEEKLY MEASUREMENTS LOG

WEIGHT _____164_____
LBS

INCHES

_34"_	_21 3/4"_	_21 1/4"_
CHEST	LEFT THIGH	RIGHT THIGH
_36"_	_9"_	_9 1/4"_
WAIST	LEFT BICEPS	RIGHT BICEPS
_38 1/2"_		
HIPS (at fullest part)		

PERSONAL NOTES

ENERGY LEVEL (circle one)
1 being "I'm so tired I can't get out of bed" and **10 being** "I could dance all night!"

1	2	3	4	5	6	7	(8)	9	10

SELF-ESTEEM/SELF-CONFIDENCE (circle one)
1 being "I can't do anything right" and **10 being** "I'm ready to change the world!"

1	2	3	4	5	6	(7)	8	9	10

Additional observations, challenges, notes:

This week, I really pushed myself on the lower-body and core exercises.
I feel it in my legs for sure! But I noticed I also felt it all week on
the sides of my abs. Even sitting at my office desk feels like a workout.

Additional observations, challenges, notes (cont'd):

I'm loving the Peachy Pork Ole from the 2-week menu and ate it twice this week! Cauliflower is surprisingly good... I probably wouldn't have touched it before trying this recipe, but now I'm definitely going to eat it more often.

It's hard to believe how much energy I've had this week, too! I focused better at work, had no problem waking up in the morning, and just feel better than usual. I hope it lasts!

PERSONAL PROFILE

I, _____,
do solemnly swear to make myself a
priority and to follow the Walk Off Weight program.

|||||||||||||||||||||||||||||||||||||||||||||||||||||||||||||||||

My goal is _____

_____

_____

Being overweight or out of shape makes me feel _____

_____

_____

I want to achieve this goal because _____

_____

_____

Achieving this goal means _____

_____

_____

With my stronger, slimmer, fitter body, I plan to _____

_____

_____

X _____
(Sign your name here.)

Now lace up your walking shoes and
get ready for a journey that's going to take
you to a healthier, happier way of life.

Starting Stats

Record these measurements before you begin the program so you have a baseline from which to assess your progress. Seeing changes in these measurements can help you to stay motivated. If the numbers aren't improving as much as you'd like, this information can help you to modify the program to maximize your results.

TODAY'S DATE/TIME	
NAME:	
AGE:	HEIGHT:
WEIGHT:	
BODY MASS INDEX (BMI):	

You can calculate your BMI using the following formula: Multiply your weight in pounds by 703. Divide that number by your height in inches. Divide that number by your height in inches again.

Example: A woman who weighs 145 pounds and is 67 inches tall (5'7") has a BMI of 22.7. A BMI of 25 or higher is considered overweight; a BMI of 30 or higher is obese. You want to aim for a healthy BMI between 18.5 and 24.9. Alternately, use our online BMI calculator in just a few quick clicks! Go to www.prevention.com, then search for "BMI calculator."

INCHES

Accurately measuring your own limbs and torso can be a challenge, so we recommend that you find a partner to help. Be sure to stand up straight, relax your arms, and follow these guidelines: Measure your chest at the fullest point of your bust. Take your waist measurement at the narrowest part of your torso, or about 2 inches above your navel. Measure your hips at the fullest part. Make sure the tape measure is parallel to the ground. Measure at the fullest part of each thigh and upper arm when arms and legs are relaxed, shoulder-width apart.

CHEST		LEFT THIGH		RIGHT THIGH	
WAIST		LEFT BICEPS		RIGHT BICEPS	
HIPS					

BLOODWORK

(Optional. Please consult your physician to have these measurements taken.)

RESTING HR		TOTAL CHOLESTEROL	
BP (SYSTOLIC)		HDL CHOLESTEROL	
BP (DIASTOLIC)		LDL CHOLESTEROL	
TRIGLYCERIDES		GLUCOSE	
OTHER			

1-MILE WALK

Map out a 1-mile route. Do your warm-up and cool-down separate from the 1-mile route so in total you'll be walking a little over a mile. During the 1-mile route, go at a pace that you feel you can maintain for the entire distance. You should be breathing heavy (about a 6 to 8 intensity level, but not panting.) Note your time below.

TOTAL TIME		MIN

Finding the Right Pace

When you start interval walking, judging your walking intensity can be tricky. Look at our intensity levels below to help you assess whether you need to speed things up, take it easy, or keep on exactly the way you're going.

ACTIVITY	INTENSITY LEVEL	PACE	HOW IT FEELS	SPEED ESTIMATES**
Inactive	1–2	Barely moving	Easy; you could do it for a very long period of time	<2.0 MPH
Easy*	3–5	Leisurely stroll	Light effort, rhythmic breathing; you can sing	2.0–3.5 MPH
Moderate	5–6	Purposeful	Some effort, breathing somewhat hard; you can talk in full sentences	3.0–4.0 MPH
Brisk	6–7	In a bit of a hurry	Hard effort, slightly breathless; you can only talk in brief phrases	3.5–4.5 MPH
Fast	7–8	Late for an appointment	Very hard effort, breathless; yes/no responses are all you can manage	4.0–5.0 MPH
Very Fast	8–9	Trying to catch a bus as it's pulling away	Maximum effort; you have no breath for talking	4.5–5.5 MPH
Sprint	10	Racing for your life	All out effort; you can't maintain it for more than a minute	5.5+ MPH

*Use this for warm-up and cool-down.

**These are only rough estimates, with the midpoint based on someone who is moderately fit. If you're just starting out, you'll probably hit each intensity level at a slower pace, closer to the lower end of the speed range or even below. If you've been walking regularly and you're very fit, you may have to walk faster, aiming toward the higher end of the range, to achieve the recommended effort levels. Pay attention to your body and do what feels right to you.

How Exercise Should Feel

Anytime you're doing something that's out of your comfort zone—which is the intention of exercise in order for your body to change—it's going to be uncomfortable. It's normal, but some symptoms aren't normal and shouldn't be ignored. Here are guidelines for how exercise should feel, what's abnormal, and what to do if you experience any of these symptoms.

NORMAL	ABNORMAL	WHAT TO DO
Heart pumping rhythmically harder and faster	Chest pain, pressure, or tightness; skipped heartbeats or palpitations	Stop immediately and call 911.
Breathing faster and harder	Difficult or uncomfortable breathing that doesn't improve when you decrease your workout intensity or stop exercising	Stop immediately and call your doctor.
Muscle soreness or burning	Sharp, shooting pain or pain in a joint	Stop and rest and ice the area. If pain persists, call your doctor.
General fatigue	Light-headedness or dizziness	Stop immediately and call your doctor.

THE STARTING LINE

What are your long-term fitness goals?

_____

_____

_____

_____

_____

_____

_____

_____

_____

_____

_____

_____

_____

WEEK 1
YOUR WORKOUT AT-A-GLANCE

DAY	ACTIVITY//WORKOUT	TOTAL
1	Basic Interval Walk I (30 min) // Lower-Body Strength Workout (15 min)	45 min
2	Toning Walk I (20 min)	20 min
3	Basic Interval Walk I (30 min) // Core Strength Workout (15 min)	45 min
4	Toning Walk I (20 min)	20 min
5	Basic Interval I (30 min) // Lower-Body Strength Workout (15 min)	45 min
6	Long Walk I (45 min) // Core Strength Workout (15 min)	60 min
7	Rest	

WHAT YOU'LL DO THIS WEEK

**3 x Basic Interval Walk I // 2 x Toning Walk I // 2 x Lower-Body Strength Workout
2 x Core Strength Workout // 1 x Long Walk I**

Workout Summary

FOR DIRECTIONS, training tips, and advice on how to perform these exercises safely and at your personal fitness level, see chapter 5 of *Walk Off Weight*.

LOWER-BODY Routine
Do 6–8 reps of the following exercises:
>> **Cross Leg Swing**
>> **One-Leg Squat**
>> **Rear Kick**
>> **Reverse Lunge**
>> **Moving Squat**

CORE Routine
>> **Plank** *(Hold once for 15 seconds)*
Do 6-8 reps of the following exercises:
>> **Tabletop Balance**
>> **Side Plank**
>> **Roll Down**
>> **Bicycle**

TECHNIQUE FOCUS: Eyes Up, Arms Up

EYES UP Good posture is essential to hit your maximum speed and feel good while you're doing it. One of the quickest ways to stand more erect is to simply look up and keep your eyes on the horizon. Bonus: You'll look slimmer, without losing a pound.

ARMS UP Bend your elbows 90 degrees and swing your arms forward and back, not out to the sides. Keep your elbows in and your hands close to your body, so they're almost skimming your sides as they swing. On the back motion, bring your hand all the way back just past your hip. As your hand comes forward, let it swing to about chest height, but don't allow it to pass the midline of your body.

BASIC INTERVAL WALK I

DURING THIS WORKOUT, focus on pushing yourself out of your comfort zone for the fast intervals. They should feel hard; this isn't supposed to be a walk in the park.

TIME	ACTIVITY	INTENSITY
0:00–5:00	Warm-Up (5 min)	3→5
5:00–6:00	Moderate (1 min)	5–6
6:00–6:30	Fast (30 sec)	7–8
6:30–7:30	Moderate (1 min)	5–6
7:30–8:00	Fast (30 sec)	7–8
8:00–9:00	Moderate (1 min)	5–6
9:00–9:30	Fast (30 sec)	7–8
9:30–10:30	Moderate (1 min)	5–6
10:30–11:00	Fast (30 sec)	7–8
11:00–12:00	Moderate (1 min)	5–6
12:00–12:30	Fast (30 sec)	7–8
12:30–13:30	Moderate (1 min)	5–6
13:30–14:00	Fast (30 sec)	7–8
14:00–15:00	Moderate (1 min)	5–6

TIME	ACTIVITY	INTENSITY
15:00–15:30	Fast (30 sec)	7–8
15:30–16:30	Moderate (1 min)	5–6
16:30–17:00	Fast (30 sec)	7–8
17:00–18:00	Moderate (1 min)	5–6
18:00–18:30	Fast (30 sec)	7–8
18:30–19:30	Moderate (1 min)	5–6
19:30–20:00	Fast (30 sec)	7–8
20:00–21:00	Moderate (1 min)	5–6
21:00–21:30	Fast (30 sec)	7–8
21:30–22:30	Moderate (1 min)	5–6
22:30–23:00	Fast (30 sec)	7–8
23:00–24:00	Moderate (1 min)	5–6
24:00–24:30	Fast (30 sec)	7–8
24:30–25:30	Moderate (1 min)	5–6
25:30–30:00	Cool-Down (4.5 min)	5→3

TONING WALK I

BETWEEN BOUTS OF BRISK WALKING, slow your pace slightly and do upper-body exercises using an elastic resistance band to tone your arms, shoulders, back, and chest while you walk off fat with this double-duty routine.

TIME	ACTIVITY	INTENSITY
0:00–4:00	Warm-Up (4 min)	3→5
4:00–4:45	Pull-Down, right arm (45 sec; 20 reps)	5–6
4:45–5:45	Brisk Walk (1 min)	6–7
5:45–6:30	Pull-Down, left arm (45 sec; 20 reps)	5–6
6:30–7:30	Brisk Walk (1 min)	6–7
7:30–8:15	Front Press (45 sec; 20 reps)	5–6
8:15–9:15	Brisk Walk (1 min)	6–7
9:15–10:00	Row, right arm (45 sec; 20 reps)	5–6
10:00–11:00	Brisk Walk (1 min)	6–7
11:00–11:45	Row, left arm (45 sec; 20 reps)	5–6
11:45–12:45	Brisk Walk (1 min)	6–7
12:45–13:30	Overhead Press (45 sec; 20 reps)	5–6
13:30–14:30	Brisk Walk (1 min)	6–7
14:30–15:15	Front Pull (45 sec; 20 reps)	5–6
15:15–16:15	Brisk Walk (1 min)	6–7
16:15–17:00	Arm Pull (45 sec; 20 reps)	5–6
17:00–18:00	Brisk Walk (1 min)	6–7
18:00–20:00	Cool-Down (2 min)	5→3

LONG WALK I

TIME	ACTIVITY	INTENSITY
0:00–5:00	Warm-Up (5 min)	3→5
5:00–40:00	Easy to Moderate Walk (35 min)	4–5
40:00–45:00	Cool-Down (5 min)	5→3

WORKOUT LOG

WORKOUTS	TIME	DURATION
	DAILY TOTAL EXERCISE TIME	

WORKOUT NOTES

How did you feel before? _____

_____

How did you feel after? _____

_____

Any obstacles? _____

_____

Major accomplishment? _____

_____

Other notes: _____

_____

PERSONAL NOTES

ENERGY LEVEL (circle one)
1 being "I'm so tired I can't get out of bed" and **10 being** "I could dance all night!"

1	2	3	4	5	6	7	8	9	10

SELF-ESTEEM/SELF-CONFIDENCE (circle one)
1 being "I can't do anything right" and **10 being** "I'm ready to change the world!"

1	2	3	4	5	6	7	8	9	10

FOOD LOG

	FOOD/DRINKS	TIME	CALORIES
Breakfast			
Lunch			
Snack			
Dinner			
Optional Snack			
		DAILY CALORIE TOTAL	

DAILY NUTRITION GOALS:	Grains/Starches ☐☐☐☐☐☐	Fruits ☐☐☐	Vegetables ☐☐☐☐☐	Dairy ☐☐☐	Healthy Fats ☐☐☐☐	Lean Proteins ☐☐☐
	Water ☑☑☐☐☐☐	Green Tea ☐☐☐	Optional (amount per day) Fiber _____ g Calcium _____ mg Vitamin D _____ IU			

BONUS TRACKER (Record your blood sugar, track your medications, gauge your hunger, or make other notes here.)

_____

_____

_____

_____

WORKOUT LOG

WORKOUTS	TIME	DURATION
	DAILY TOTAL EXERCISE TIME	

WORKOUT NOTES

How did you feel before? _____

_____

How did you feel after? _____

_____

Any obstacles? _____

_____

Major accomplishment? _____

_____

Other notes: _____

_____

PERSONAL NOTES

ENERGY LEVEL (circle one)
1 being "I'm so tired I can't get out of bed" and **10 being** "I could dance all night!"

1	2	3	4	5	6	7	8	9	10

SELF-ESTEEM/SELF-CONFIDENCE (circle one)
1 being "I can't do anything right" and **10 being** "I'm ready to change the world!"

1	2	3	4	5	6	7	8	9	10

FOOD LOG

	FOOD/DRINKS	TIME	CALORIES
Breakfast			
Lunch			
Snack			
Dinner			
Optional Snack			
		DAILY CALORIE TOTAL	

DAILY NUTRITION GOALS:	Grains/Starches ☐☐☐☐☐☐	Fruits ☐☐☐	Vegetables ☐☐☐☐☐	Dairy ☐☐☐	Healthy Fats ☐☐☐☐	Lean Proteins ☐☐☐
	Water ☒☒☒☒☒	Green Tea ☐☐☐	Optional (amount per day) Fiber _____ g Calcium _____ mg Vitamin D _____ IU			

BONUS TRACKER (Record your blood sugar, track your medications, gauge your hunger, or make other notes here.)

_____

_____

_____

_____

WORKOUT LOG

WORKOUTS	TIME	DURATION
		40 min
		20 min
	DAILY TOTAL EXERCISE TIME	

WORKOUT NOTES

How did you feel before? _____

_____

How did you feel after? _____

_____

Any obstacles? _____

_____

Major accomplishment? _____

_____

Other notes: _____

_____

PERSONAL NOTES

ENERGY LEVEL (circle one)
1 being "I'm so tired I can't get out of bed" and **10 being** "I could dance all night!"

1	2	3	4	5	6	7	8	9	10

SELF-ESTEEM/SELF-CONFIDENCE (circle one)
1 being "I can't do anything right" and **10 being** "I'm ready to change the world!"

1	2	3	4	5	6	7	8	9	10

FOOD LOG

	FOOD/DRINKS	TIME	CALORIES
Breakfast			
Lunch			
Snack			
Dinner			
Optional Snack			
	DAILY CALORIE TOTAL		

DAILY NUTRITION GOALS:	Grains/Starches ☐☐☐☐☐☐	Fruits ☐☐☐	Vegetables ☐☐☐☐☐	Dairy ☐☐☐	Healthy Fats ☐☐☐☐	Lean Proteins ☐☐☐
	Water ☐☐☐☐☐	Green Tea ☐☐☐	*Optional* (amount per day) Fiber _____ g Calcium _____ mg **Vitamin D** _____ IU			

BONUS TRACKER *(Record your blood sugar, track your medications, gauge your hunger, or make other notes here.)*

_____

_____

_____

_____

WORKOUT LOG

WORKOUTS	TIME	DURATION
	DAILY TOTAL EXERCISE TIME	

WORKOUT NOTES

How did you feel before? _____

_____

How did you feel after? _____

_____

Any obstacles? _____

_____

Major accomplishment? _____

_____

Other notes: _____

_____

PERSONAL NOTES

ENERGY LEVEL (circle one)
1 being "I'm so tired I can't get out of bed" and **10 being** "I could dance all night!"

1	2	3	4	5	6	7	8	9	10

SELF-ESTEEM/SELF-CONFIDENCE (circle one)
1 being "I can't do anything right" and **10 being** "I'm ready to change the world!"

1	2	3	4	5	6	7	8	9	10

FOOD LOG

	FOOD/DRINKS	TIME	CALORIES
Breakfast			
Lunch			
Snack			
Dinner			
Optional Snack			
		DAILY CALORIE TOTAL	

DAILY NUTRITION GOALS:	Grains/Starches	Fruits	Vegetables	Dairy	Healthy Fats	Lean Proteins
	☐☐☐☐☐☐	☐☐☐	☐☐☐☐☐	☐☐☐	☐☐☐☐	☐☐☐
	Water	Green Tea	*Optional* (amount per day)			
	☐☐☐☐☐	☐☐☐	Fiber _____ g Calcium _____ mg Vitamin D _____ IU			

BONUS TRACKER *(Record your blood sugar, track your medications, gauge your hunger, or make other notes here.)*

_____

_____

_____

_____

WORKOUT LOG

WORKOUTS	TIME	DURATION
	DAILY TOTAL EXERCISE TIME	

WORKOUT NOTES

How did you feel before? _____

_____

How did you feel after? _____

_____

Any obstacles? _____

_____

Major accomplishment? _____

_____

Other notes: _____

_____

PERSONAL NOTES

ENERGY LEVEL (circle one)
1 being "I'm so tired I can't get out of bed" and **10 being** "I could dance all night!"

1	2	3	4	5	6	7	8	9	10

SELF-ESTEEM/SELF-CONFIDENCE (circle one)
1 being "I can't do anything right" and **10 being** "I'm ready to change the world!"

1	2	3	4	5	6	7	8	9	10

FOOD LOG

	FOOD/DRINKS	TIME	CALORIES
Breakfast			
Lunch			
Snack			
Dinner			
Optional Snack			
		DAILY CALORIE TOTAL	

DAILY NUTRITION GOALS:	Grains/Starches	Fruits	Vegetables	Dairy	Healthy Fats	Lean Proteins
	☐☐☐☐☐☐	☐☐☐	☐☐☐☐☐	☐☐☐	☐☐☐☐	☐☐☐
	Water	Green Tea	Optional (amount per day)			
	☐☐☐☐☐	☐☐☐	Fiber _____ g Calcium _____ mg Vitamin D _____ IU			

BONUS TRACKER (*Record your blood sugar, track your medications, gauge your hunger, or make other notes here.*)

_____

_____

_____

_____

WORKOUT LOG

WORKOUTS	TIME	DURATION
	DAILY TOTAL EXERCISE TIME	

WORKOUT NOTES

How did you feel before? _____

_____

How did you feel after? _____

_____

Any obstacles? _____

_____

Major accomplishment? _____

_____

Other notes: _____

_____

PERSONAL NOTES

ENERGY LEVEL (circle one)
1 being "I'm so tired I can't get out of bed" and **10 being** "I could dance all night!"

1	2	3	4	5	6	7	8	9	10

SELF-ESTEEM/SELF-CONFIDENCE (circle one)
1 being "I can't do anything right" and **10 being** "I'm ready to change the world!"

1	2	3	4	5	6	7	8	9	10

FOOD LOG

	FOOD/DRINKS	TIME	CALORIES
Breakfast			
Lunch			
Snack			
Dinner			
Optional Snack			
	DAILY CALORIE TOTAL		

DAILY NUTRITION GOALS:	Grains/Starches	Fruits	Vegetables	Dairy	Healthy Fats	Lean Proteins
	☐☐☐☐☐☐	☐☐☐	☐☐☐☐☐	☐☐☐	☐☐☐☐	☐☐☐
	Water	Green Tea	Optional (amount per day)			
	☐☐☐☐☐	☐☐☐	Fiber _____ g Calcium _____ mg Vitamin D _____ IU			

BONUS TRACKER (*Record your blood sugar, track your medications, gauge your hunger, or make other notes here.*)

_____

_____

_____

_____

WORKOUT LOG

WORKOUTS	TIME	DURATION
	DAILY TOTAL EXERCISE TIME	

WORKOUT NOTES

How did you feel before? _____

_____

How did you feel after? _____

_____

Any obstacles? _____

_____

Major accomplishment? _____

_____

Other notes: _____

_____

PERSONAL NOTES

ENERGY LEVEL (circle one)
1 being "I'm so tired I can't get out of bed" and **10 being** "I could dance all night!"

1	2	3	4	5	6	7	8	9	10

SELF-ESTEEM/SELF-CONFIDENCE (circle one)
1 being "I can't do anything right" and **10 being** "I'm ready to change the world!"

1	2	3	4	5	6	7	8	9	10

FOOD LOG

	FOOD/DRINKS	TIME	CALORIES
Breakfast			
Lunch			
Snack			
Dinner			
Optional Snack			
		DAILY CALORIE TOTAL	

DAILY NUTRITION GOALS:	Grains/Starches ☐☐☐☐☐☐	Fruits ☐☐☐	Vegetables ☐☐☐☐☐	Dairy ☐☐☐	Healthy Fats ☐☐☐☐	Lean Proteins ☐☐☐
	Water ☐☐☐☐☐	Green Tea ☐☐☐	*Optional* (amount per day) Fiber _____ g **Calcium** _____mg **Vitamin D** _____IU			

BONUS TRACKER *(Record your blood sugar, track your medications, gauge your hunger, or make other notes here.)*

_____

_____

_____

_____

DATE/TIME _____

WEEKLY MEASUREMENTS LOG

WEIGHT _____
LBS

INCHES _____ _____ _____
CHEST LEFT THIGH RIGHT THIGH

_____ _____ _____
WAIST LEFT BICEPS RIGHT BICEPS

_____
HIPS (at fullest part)

PERSONAL NOTES
ENERGY LEVEL (circle one)
1 being "I'm so tired I can't get out of bed" and **10 being** "I could dance all night!"

1	2	3	4	5	6	7	8	9	10

SELF-ESTEEM/SELF-CONFIDENCE (circle one)
1 being "I can't do anything right" and **10 being** "I'm ready to change the world!"

1	2	3	4	5	6	7	8	9	10

Additional observations, challenges, notes:

_____

_____

_____

_____

_____

Additional observations, challenges, notes (cont'd):

_____

_____

_____

_____

_____

_____

_____

_____

_____

_____

_____

_____

_____

_____

_____

_____

_____

_____

_____

_____

_____

_____

_____

_____

_____

_____

WEEK 2
YOUR WORKOUT AT-A-GLANCE

DAY	ACTIVITY//WORKOUT	TOTAL
1	Basic Interval Walk I (30 min) // Lower-Body Strength Workout (15 min)	45 min
2	Toning Walk I (20 min)	20 min
3	Basic Interval Walk I (30 min) // Core Strength Workout (15 min)	45 min
4	Toning Walk I (20 min)	20 min
5	Basic Interval Walk I (30 min) // Lower-Body Strength Workout (15 min)	45 min
6	Long Walk II (60 min) // Core Strength Workout (15 min)	75 min
7	Rest	

|||||||||||||||||||||||||||||||||||||||||||||||||||||||||||||||||||||||||||||||||||||||||||||||||||

WHAT YOU'LL DO THIS WEEK

**3 x Basic Interval Walk I // 2 x Toning Walk I // 2 x Lower-Body Strength Workout
2 x Core Strength Workout // 1 x Long Walk II**

|||||||||||||||||||||||||||||||||||||||||||||||||||||||||||||||||||||||||||||||||||||||||||||||||||

Workout Summary

FOR DIRECTIONS, training tips, and advice on how to perform these exercises safely and at your personal fitness level, see chapter 5 of *Walk Off Weight*.

LOWER-BODY Routine
Do 8-10 reps of the following exercises:
>> **Cross Leg Swing**
>> **One-Leg Squat**
>> **Rear Kick**
>> **Reverse Lunge**
>> **Moving Squat**

CORE Routine
>> **Plank** *(Hold once for 30 seconds)*
Do 8-10 reps of the following exercises:
>> **Tabletop Balance**
>> **Side Plank**
>> **Roll Down**
>> **Bicycle**

TECHNIQUE FOCUS: Up, Roll, Push

The heel-to-toe roll is key to powering a strong, quick stride.
TOES UP As you step, focus on landing on your heel with your toes up in the air. If you hear slapping as you walk, that means you're landing flat-footed.
ROLL The next phase of the action is rolling from your heel to your toes as smoothly as possible.
PUSH OFF Finally, push off with your toes as if you're kicking sand behind you.

BASIC INTERVAL WALK I

TIME	ACTIVITY	INTENSITY	TIME	ACTIVITY	INTENSITY
0:00–5:00	Warm-Up (5 min)	3➜5	15:00–15:30	Fast (30 sec)	7–8
5:00–6:00	Moderate (1 min)	5–6	15:30–16:30	Moderate (1 min)	5–6
6:00–6:30	Fast (30 sec)	7–8	16:30–17:00	Fast (30 sec)	7–8
6:30–7:30	Moderate (1 min)	5–6	17:00–18:00	Moderate (1 min)	5–6
7:30–8:00	Fast (30 sec)	7–8	18:00–18:30	Fast (30 sec)	7–8
8:00–9:00	Moderate (1 min)	5–6	18:30–19:30	Moderate (1 min)	5–6
9:00–9:30	Fast (30 sec)	7–8	19:30–20:00	Fast (30 sec)	7–8
9:30–10:30	Moderate (1 min)	5–6	20:00–21:00	Moderate (1 min)	5–6
10:30–11:00	Fast (30 sec)	7–8	21:00–21:30	Fast (30 sec)	7–8
11:00–12:00	Moderate (1 min)	5–6	21:30–22:30	Moderate (1 min)	5–6
12:00–12:30	Fast (30 sec)	7–8	22:30–23:00	Fast (30 sec)	7–8
12:30–13:30	Moderate (1 min)	5–6	23:00–24:00	Moderate (1 min)	5–6
13:30–14:00	Fast (30 sec)	7–8	24:00–24:30	Fast (30 sec)	7–8
14:00–15:00	Moderate (1 min)	5–6	24:30–25:30	Moderate (1 min)	5–6
			25:30–30:00	Cool-Down (4.5 min)	5➜3

TONING WALK I

TIME	ACTIVITY	INTENSITY
0:00–4:00	Warm-Up (4 min)	3➜5
4:00–4:45	Pull-Down, right arm (45 sec; 20 reps)	5–6
4:45–5:45	Brisk Walk (1 min)	6–7
5:45–6:30	Pull-Down, left arm (45 sec; 20 reps)	5–6
6:30–7:30	Brisk Walk (1 min)	6–7
7:30–8:15	Front Press (45 sec; 20 reps)	5–6
8:15–9:15	Brisk Walk (1 min)	6–7
9:15–10:00	Row, right arm (45 sec; 20 reps)	5–6
10:00–11:00	Brisk Walk (1 min)	6–7
11:00–11:45	Row, left arm (45 sec; 20 reps)	5–6
11:45–12:45	Brisk Walk (1 min)	6–7
12:45–13:30	Overhead Press (45 sec; 20 reps)	5–6
13:30–14:30	Brisk Walk (1 min)	6–7
14:30–15:15	Front Pull (45 sec; 20 reps)	5–6
15:15–16:15	Brisk Walk (1 min)	6–7
16:15–17:00	Arm Pull (45 sec; 20 reps)	5–6
17:00–18:00	Brisk Walk (1 min)	6–7
18:00–20:00	Cool-Down (2 min)	5➜3

LONG WALK II

TIME	ACTIVITY	INTENSITY
0:00–5:00	Warm-Up (5 min)	3➜5
5:00–55:00	Easy to Moderate Walk (50 min)	4–5
55:00–60:00	Cool-Down (5 min)	5➜3

WORKOUT LOG

WORKOUTS	TIME	DURATION
	DAILY TOTAL EXERCISE TIME	

WORKOUT NOTES

How did you feel before? _____

_____

How did you feel after? _____

_____

Any obstacles? _____

_____

Major accomplishment? _____

_____

Other notes: _____

_____

PERSONAL NOTES

ENERGY LEVEL (circle one)
1 being "I'm so tired I can't get out of bed" and **10 being** "I could dance all night!"

1	2	3	4	5	6	7	8	9	10

SELF-ESTEEM/SELF-CONFIDENCE (circle one)
1 being "I can't do anything right" and **10 being** "I'm ready to change the world!"

1	2	3	4	5	6	7	8	9	10

FOOD LOG

	FOOD/DRINKS	TIME	CALORIES
Breakfast			
Lunch			
Snack			
Dinner			
Optional Snack			
		DAILY CALORIE TOTAL	

DAILY NUTRITION GOALS:	Grains/Starches	Fruits	Vegetables	Dairy	Healthy Fats	Lean Proteins
	☐☐☐☐☐☐	☐☐☐	☐☐☐☐☐	☐☐☐	☐☐☐☐	☐☐☐
	Water	Green Tea	Optional (amount per day)			
	☐☐☐☐☐	☐☐☐	Fiber _____ g Calcium _____ mg Vitamin D _____ IU			

BONUS TRACKER (*Record your blood sugar, track your medications, gauge your hunger, or make other notes here.*)

_____

_____

_____

_____

WORKOUT LOG

WORKOUTS	TIME	DURATION
	DAILY TOTAL EXERCISE TIME	

WORKOUT NOTES

How did you feel before? _____

_____

How did you feel after? _____

_____

Any obstacles? _____

_____

Major accomplishment? _____

_____

Other notes: _____

_____

PERSONAL NOTES

ENERGY LEVEL (circle one)
1 being "I'm so tired I can't get out of bed" and **10 being** "I could dance all night!"

1	2	3	4	5	6	7	8	9	10

SELF-ESTEEM/SELF-CONFIDENCE (circle one)
1 being "I can't do anything right" and **10 being** "I'm ready to change the world!"

1	2	3	4	5	6	7	8	9	10

PHASE 1 WALK OFF WEIGHT

FOOD LOG

	FOOD/DRINKS	TIME	CALORIES
Breakfast			
Lunch			
Snack			
Dinner			
Optional Snack			
	DAILY CALORIE TOTAL		

DAILY NUTRITION GOALS:

Grains/Starches	Fruits	Vegetables	Dairy	Healthy Fats	Lean Proteins
☐☐☐☐☐☐	☐☐☐	☐☐☐☐☐	☐☐☐	☐☐☐☐	☐☐☐

Water ☐☐☐☐☐ Green Tea ☐☐☐ Optional (amount per day)
Fiber ____ g Calcium ____ mg Vitamin D ____ IU

BONUS TRACKER (Record your blood sugar, track your medications, gauge your hunger, or make other notes here.)

_____
_____
_____
_____

37

WORKOUT LOG

WORKOUTS	TIME	DURATION
	DAILY TOTAL EXERCISE TIME	

WORKOUT NOTES

How did you feel before? _____

_____

How did you feel after? _____

_____

Any obstacles? _____

_____

Major accomplishment? _____

_____

Other notes: _____

_____

PERSONAL NOTES

ENERGY LEVEL (circle one)
1 being "I'm so tired I can't get out of bed" and **10 being** "I could dance all night!"

1	2	3	4	5	6	7	8	9	10

SELF-ESTEEM/SELF-CONFIDENCE (circle one)
1 being "I can't do anything right" and **10 being** "I'm ready to change the world!"

1	2	3	4	5	6	7	8	9	10

FOOD LOG

	FOOD/DRINKS	TIME	CALORIES
Breakfast			
Lunch			
Snack			
Dinner			
Optional Snack			
	DAILY CALORIE TOTAL		

DAILY NUTRITION GOALS:	Grains/Starches	Fruits	Vegetables	Dairy	Healthy Fats	Lean Proteins
	☐☐☐☐☐☐	☐☐☐	☐☐☐☐☐	☐☐☐	☐☐☐☐	☐☐☐
	Water	Green Tea	Optional (amount per day)			
	☐☐☐☐☐	☐☐☐	Fiber ____g Calcium ____mg **Vitamin D** ____IU			

BONUS TRACKER *(Record your blood sugar, track your medications, gauge your hunger, or make other notes here.)*

_____

_____

_____

_____

WORKOUT LOG

WORKOUTS	TIME	DURATION
	DAILY TOTAL EXERCISE TIME	

WORKOUT NOTES

How did you feel before? _____

_____

How did you feel after? _____

_____

Any obstacles? _____

_____

Major accomplishment? _____

_____

Other notes: _____

_____

PERSONAL NOTES

ENERGY LEVEL (circle one)
1 being "I'm so tired I can't get out of bed" and **10 being** "I could dance all night!"

1	2	3	4	5	6	7	8	9	10

SELF-ESTEEM/SELF-CONFIDENCE (circle one)
1 being "I can't do anything right" and **10 being** "I'm ready to change the world!"

1	2	3	4	5	6	7	8	9	10

PHASE 1 WALK OFF WEIGHT

FOOD LOG

	FOOD/DRINKS	TIME	CALORIES
Breakfast			
Lunch			
Snack			
Dinner			
Optional Snack			
	DAILY CALORIE TOTAL		

DAILY NUTRITION GOALS:	Grains/Starches ▢▢▢▢▢▢	Fruits ▢▢▢	Vegetables ▢▢▢▢▢	Dairy ▢▢▢	Healthy Fats ▢▢▢▢	Lean Proteins ▢▢▢
	Water ▢▢▢▢▢	Green Tea ▢▢▢	Optional (amount per day) Fiber _____g Calcium _____mg Vitamin D _____IU			

BONUS TRACKER (Record your blood sugar, track your medications, gauge your hunger, or make other notes here.)

_____

_____

_____

_____

WORKOUT LOG

WORKOUTS	TIME	DURATION
	DAILY TOTAL EXERCISE TIME	

WORKOUT NOTES

How did you feel before? _____

_____

How did you feel after? _____

_____

Any obstacles? _____

_____

Major accomplishment? _____

_____

Other notes: _____

_____

PERSONAL NOTES

ENERGY LEVEL (circle one)
1 being "I'm so tired I can't get out of bed" and **10 being** "I could dance all night!"

1	2	3	4	5	6	7	8	9	10

SELF-ESTEEM/SELF-CONFIDENCE (circle one)
1 being "I can't do anything right" and **10 being** "I'm ready to change the world!"

1	2	3	4	5	6	7	8	9	10

FOOD LOG

	FOOD/DRINKS	TIME	CALORIES
Breakfast			
Lunch			
Snack			
Dinner			
Optional Snack			
	DAILY CALORIE TOTAL		

DAILY NUTRITION GOALS:	Grains/Starches ☐☐☐☐☐☐	Fruits ☐☐☐	Vegetables ☐☐☐☐☐	Dairy ☐☐☐	Healthy Fats ☐☐☐☐	Lean Proteins ☐☐☐
	Water ☐☐☐☐☐	Green Tea ☐☐☐	Optional (amount per day) Fiber _____ g Calcium _____ mg Vitamin D _____ IU			

BONUS TRACKER (*Record your blood sugar, track your medications, gauge your hunger, or make other notes here.*)

_____

_____

_____

_____

WORKOUT LOG

WORKOUTS	TIME	DURATION
	DAILY TOTAL EXERCISE TIME	

WORKOUT NOTES

How did you feel before? _____

_____

How did you feel after? _____

_____

Any obstacles? _____

_____

Major accomplishment? _____

_____

Other notes: _____

_____

PERSONAL NOTES

ENERGY LEVEL (circle one)
1 being "I'm so tired I can't get out of bed" and **10 being** "I could dance all night!"

1	2	3	4	5	6	7	8	9	10

SELF-ESTEEM/SELF-CONFIDENCE (circle one)
1 being "I can't do anything right" and **10 being** "I'm ready to change the world!"

1	2	3	4	5	6	7	8	9	10

FOOD LOG

	FOOD/DRINKS	TIME	CALORIES
Breakfast			
Lunch			
Snack			
Dinner			
Optional Snack			
		DAILY CALORIE TOTAL	

DAILY NUTRITION GOALS:	Grains/Starches	Fruits	Vegetables	Dairy	Healthy Fats	Lean Proteins
	☐☐☐☐☐☐	☐☐☐	☐☐☐☐☐	☐☐☐	☐☐☐☐	☐☐☐
	Water	Green Tea	Optional (amount per day)			
	☐☐☐☐☐	☐☐☐	Fiber _____ g Calcium _____ mg Vitamin D _____ IU			

BONUS TRACKER (*Record your blood sugar, track your medications, gauge your hunger, or make other notes here.*)

_____

_____

_____

_____

WORKOUT LOG

WORKOUTS	TIME	DURATION
	DAILY TOTAL EXERCISE TIME	

WORKOUT NOTES

How did you feel before? _____

_____

How did you feel after? _____

_____

Any obstacles? _____

_____

Major accomplishment? _____

_____

Other notes: _____

_____

PERSONAL NOTES

ENERGY LEVEL (circle one)
1 being "I'm so tired I can't get out of bed" and **10 being** "I could dance all night!"

1	2	3	4	5	6	7	8	9	10

SELF-ESTEEM/SELF-CONFIDENCE (circle one)
1 being "I can't do anything right" and **10 being** "I'm ready to change the world!"

1	2	3	4	5	6	7	8	9	10

FOOD LOG

	FOOD/DRINKS	TIME	CALORIES
Breakfast			
Lunch			
Snack			
Dinner			
Optional Snack			
	DAILY CALORIE TOTAL		

DAILY NUTRITION GOALS:	Grains/Starches ☐☐☐☐☐☐	Fruits ☐☐☐	Vegetables ☐☐☐☐☐	Dairy ☐☐☐	Healthy Fats ☐☐☐☐	Lean Proteins ☐☐☐
	Water ☐☐☐☐☐	Green Tea ☐☐☐	*Optional* (amount per day) Fiber _____g Calcium _____mg **Vitamin D** _____IU			

BONUS TRACKER *(Record your blood sugar, track your medications, gauge your hunger, or make other notes here.)*

_____

_____

_____

_____

WEEKLY MEASUREMENTS LOG

WEIGHT _____
LBS

INCHES _____   _____   _____
CHEST   LEFT THIGH   RIGHT THIGH

_____   _____   _____
WAIST   LEFT BICEPS   RIGHT BICEPS

_____
HIPS (at fullest part)

PERSONAL NOTES
ENERGY LEVEL (circle one)
1 being "I'm so tired I can't get out of bed" and **10 being** "I could dance all night!"

1	2	3	4	5	6	7	8	9	10

SELF-ESTEEM/SELF-CONFIDENCE (circle one)
1 being "I can't do anything right" and **10 being** "I'm ready to change the world!"

1	2	3	4	5	6	7	8	9	10

Additional observations, challenges, notes:

_____

_____

_____

_____

_____

Additional observations, challenges, notes (cont'd):

_____

_____

_____

_____

_____

_____

_____

_____

_____

_____

_____

_____

_____

_____

_____

_____

_____

_____

_____

_____

_____

_____

_____

_____

WEEK 3
YOUR WORKOUT AT-A-GLANCE

DAY	ACTIVITY//WORKOUT	TOTAL
1	Basic Interval Walk II (45 min) // Lower-Body Strength Workout (15 min)	60 min
2	Toning Walk II (25 min)	25 min
3	Basic Interval Walk II (45 min)// Core Strength Workout (15 min)	60 min
4	Toning Walk II (25 min)	25 min
5	Basic Interval Walk II (45 min) // Lower-Body Strength Workout (15 min)	60 min
6	Long Walk III (75 min) // Core Strength Workout (15 min)	90 min
7	Rest	

|||||||||||||||||||||||||||||||||||||||||||||||||||||||||||||||||||||||||||||||||

WHAT YOU'LL **DO THIS WEEK**

3 x Basic Interval Walk II // **2 x Toning Walk II** // **2 x Lower-Body Strength Workout**
2 x Core Strength Workout // **1 x Long Walk III**

|||||||||||||||||||||||||||||||||||||||||||||||||||||||||||||||||||||||||||||||||

Workout Summary

FOR DIRECTIONS, training tips, and advice on how to perform these exercises safely and at your personal fitness level, see chapter 5 of *Walk Off Weight*.

LOWER-BODY Routine
Do 10-12 reps of the following exercises:
>> **Cross Leg Swing**
>> **One-Leg Squat**
>> **Rear Kicks**
>> **ReverseLunge**
>> **Moving Squats**

CORE Routine
>> **Plank** (*Hold once for 45 seconds*)
Do 10-12 reps of the following exercises:
>> **Tabletop Balance**
>> **Side Plank**
>> **Roll Down**
>> **Bicycle**

TECHNIQUE FOCUS: Strong Push-Off

You should have been thinking about this a little bit last week, as you focused on your heel-to-toe roll. Because this part of each step is critical to powering your speed, pay attention to it again this week. The key to getting maximum acceleration is to wait until your foot is behind you before you push off. You should have a longer stride behind you than in front of you. Then think of lifting your heel as you push off so someone who is walking behind you could see the sole of your shoe.

BASIC INTERVAL WALK II

TIME	ACTIVITY	INTENSITY	TIME	ACTIVITY	INTENSITY
0:00–5:00	Warm-Up (5 min)	3→5	22:30–23:00	Fast (30 sec)	7–8
5:00–6:00	Moderate (1 min)	5–6	23:00–24:00	Moderate (1 min)	5–6
6:00–6:30	Fast (30 sec)	7–8	24:00–24:30	Fast (30 sec)	7–8
6:30–7:30	Moderate (1 min)	5–6	24:30–25:30	Moderate (1 min)	5–6
7:30–8:00	Fast (30 sec)	7–8	25:30–26:00	Fast (30 sec)	7–8
8:00–9:00	Moderate (1 min)	5–6	26:00–27:00	Moderate (1 min)	5–6
9:00–9:30	Fast (30 sec)	7–8	27:00–27:30	Fast (30 sec)	7–8
9:30–10:30	Moderate (1 min)	5–6	27:30–28:30	Moderate (1 min)	5–6
10:30–11:00	Fast (30 sec)	7–8	28:30–29:00	Fast (30 sec)	7–8
11:00–12:00	Moderate (1 min)	5–6	29:00–30:00	Moderate (1 min)	5–6
12:00–12:30	Fast (30 sec)	7–8	30:00–30:30	Fast (30 sec)	7–8
12:30–13:30	Moderate (1 min)	5–6	30:30–31:30	Moderate (1 min)	5–6
13:30–14:00	Fast (30 sec)	7–8	31:30–32:00	Fast (30 sec)	7–8
14:00–15:00	Moderate (1 min)	5–6	32:00–33:00	Moderate (1 min)	5–6
15:00–15:30	Fast (30 sec)	7–8	33:00–33:30	Fast (30 sec)	7–8
15:30–16:30	Moderate (1 min)	5–6	33:30–34:30	Moderate (1 min)	5–6
16:30–17:00	Fast (30 sec)	7–8	34:30–35:00	Fast (30 sec)	7–8
17:00–18:00	Moderate (1 min)	5–6	35:00–36:00	Moderate (1 min)	5–6
18:00–18:30	Fast (30 sec)	7–8	36:00–36:30	Fast (30 sec)	7–8
18:30–19:30	Moderate (1 min)	5–6	36:30–37:30	Moderate (1 min)	5–6
19:30–20:00	Fast (30 sec)	7–8	37:30–38:00	Fast (30 sec)	7–8
20:00–21:00	Moderate (1 min)	5–6	38:00–39:00	Moderate (1 min)	5–6
21:00–21:30	Fast (30 sec)	7–8	39:00–39:30	Fast (30 sec)	7–8
21:30–22:30	Moderate (1 min)	5–6	39:30–40:30	Moderate (1 min)	5–6
			40:30–45:00	Cool-Down (4.5 min)	5→3

TONING WALK II

TIME	ACTIVITY	INTENSITY	TIME	ACTIVITY	INTENSITY
0:00–5:00	Warm-Up (5 min)	3→5	13:00–14:00	Row, left arm (1 min; 30 reps)	5–6
5:00–6:00	Pull-Down, right arm (1 min; 30 reps)	5–6	14:00–15:00	Brisk Walk (1 min)	6–7
6:00–7:00	Brisk Walk (1 min)	6–7	15:00–16:00	Overhead Press (1 min; 30 reps)	5–6
7:00–8:00	Pull-Down, left arm (1 min; 30 reps)	5–6	16:00–17:00	Brisk Walk (1 min)	6–7
8:00–9:00	Brisk Walk (1 min)	6–7	17:00–18:00	Front Pull (1 min; 30 reps)	5–6
9:00–10:00	Front Press (1 min; 30 reps)	5–6	18:00–19:00	Brisk Walk (1 min)	6–7
10:00–11:00	Brisk Walk (1 min)	6–7	19:00–20:00	Arm Pull (1 min; 30 reps)	5–6
11:00–12:00	Row, right arm (1 min; 30 reps)	5–6	20:00–21:00	Brisk Walk (1 min)	6–7
12:00–13:00	Brisk Walk (1 min)	6–7	21:00–25:00	Cool-Down (4 min)	5→3

LONG WALK III

TIME	ACTIVITY	INTENSITY
0:00–5:00	Warm-Up (5 min)	3→5
5:00–70:00	Easy to Moderate Walk (65 min)	4–5
70:00–75:00	Cool-Down (5 min)	5→3

WORKOUT LOG

WORKOUTS	TIME	DURATION
	DAILY TOTAL EXERCISE TIME	

WORKOUT NOTES

How did you feel before? _____

_____

How did you feel after? _____

_____

Any obstacles? _____

_____

Major accomplishment? _____

_____

Other notes: _____

_____

PERSONAL NOTES

ENERGY LEVEL (circle one)
1 being "I'm so tired I can't get out of bed" and **10 being** "I could dance all night!"

1	2	3	4	5	6	7	8	9	10

SELF-ESTEEM/SELF-CONFIDENCE (circle one)
1 being "I can't do anything right" and **10 being** "I'm ready to change the world!"

1	2	3	4	5	6	7	8	9	10

FOOD LOG

	FOOD/DRINKS	TIME	CALORIES
Breakfast			
Lunch			
Snack			
Dinner			
Optional Snack			
		DAILY CALORIE TOTAL	

DAILY NUTRITION GOALS:	Grains/Starches ☐☐☐☐☐☐	Fruits ☐☐☐	Vegetables ☐☐☐☐☐	Dairy ☐☐☐	Healthy Fats ☐☐☐☐	Lean Proteins ☐☐☐
	Water ☐☐☐☐☐	Green Tea ☐☐☐	*Optional* (amount per day) Fiber _____g Calcium _____mg Vitamin D _____IU			

BONUS TRACKER *(Record your blood sugar, track your medications, gauge your hunger, or make other notes here.)*

_____

_____

_____

_____

WORKOUT LOG

WORKOUTS	TIME	DURATION
	DAILY TOTAL EXERCISE TIME	

WORKOUT NOTES

How did you feel before? _____

_____

How did you feel after? _____

_____

Any obstacles? _____

_____

Major accomplishment? _____

_____

Other notes: _____

_____

PERSONAL NOTES

ENERGY LEVEL (circle one)
1 being "I'm so tired I can't get out of bed" and **10 being** "I could dance all night!"

1	2	3	4	5	6	7	8	9	10

SELF-ESTEEM/SELF-CONFIDENCE (circle one)
1 being "I can't do anything right" and **10 being** "I'm ready to change the world!"

1	2	3	4	5	6	7	8	9	10

FOOD LOG

	FOOD/DRINKS	TIME	CALORIES
Breakfast			
Lunch			
Snack			
Dinner			
Optional Snack			
		DAILY CALORIE TOTAL	

DAILY NUTRITION GOALS:	Grains/Starches ☐☐☐☐☐☐	Fruits ☐☐☐	Vegetables ☐☐☐☐☐	Dairy ☐☐☐	Healthy Fats ☐☐☐☐	Lean Proteins ☐☐☐
	Water ☐☐☐☐☐	Green Tea ☐☐☐	*Optional* (amount per day) Fiber _____ g Calcium _____ mg **Vitamin D** _____ IU			

BONUS TRACKER *(Record your blood sugar, track your medications, gauge your hunger, or make other notes here.)*

_____

_____

_____

_____

WORKOUT LOG

WORKOUTS	TIME	DURATION
	DAILY TOTAL EXERCISE TIME	

WORKOUT NOTES

How did you feel before? _____

_____

How did you feel after? _____

_____

Any obstacles? _____

_____

Major accomplishment? _____

_____

Other notes: _____

_____

PERSONAL NOTES

ENERGY LEVEL (circle one)
1 being "I'm so tired I can't get out of bed" and **10 being** "I could dance all night!"

1	2	3	4	5	6	7	8	9	10

SELF-ESTEEM/SELF-CONFIDENCE (circle one)
1 being "I can't do anything right" and **10 being** "I'm ready to change the world!"

1	2	3	4	5	6	7	8	9	10

FOOD LOG

	FOOD/DRINKS	TIME	CALORIES
Breakfast			
Lunch			
Snack			
Dinner			
Optional Snack			
		DAILY CALORIE TOTAL	

DAILY NUTRITION GOALS:

Grains/Starches	Fruits	Vegetables	Dairy	Healthy Fats	Lean Proteins
☐☐☐☐☐☐	☐☐☐	☐☐☐☐☐	☐☐☐	☐☐☐☐	☐☐☐

Water	Green Tea	Optional (amount per day)
☐☐☐☐☐	☐☐☐	Fiber _____ g Calcium _____ mg Vitamin D _____ IU

BONUS TRACKER (*Record your blood sugar, track your medications, gauge your hunger, or make other notes here.*)

_____

_____

_____

_____

WORKOUT LOG

WORKOUTS	TIME	DURATION
	DAILY TOTAL EXERCISE TIME	

WORKOUT NOTES

How did you feel before? _____

_____

How did you feel after? _____

_____

Any obstacles? _____

_____

Major accomplishment? _____

_____

Other notes: _____

_____

PERSONAL NOTES

ENERGY LEVEL (circle one)
1 being "I'm so tired I can't get out of bed" and **10 being** "I could dance all night!"

1	2	3	4	5	6	7	8	9	10

SELF-ESTEEM/SELF-CONFIDENCE (circle one)
1 being "I can't do anything right" and **10 being** "I'm ready to change the world!"

1	2	3	4	5	6	7	8	9	10

FOOD LOG

	FOOD/DRINKS	TIME	CALORIES
Breakfast			
Lunch			
Snack			
Dinner			
Optional Snack			
	DAILY CALORIE TOTAL		

DAILY NUTRITION GOALS:	Grains/Starches ☐☐☐☐☐☐	Fruits ☐☐☐	Vegetables ☐☐☐☐☐	Dairy ☐☐☐	Healthy Fats ☐☐☐☐	Lean Proteins ☐☐☐
	Water ☐☐☐☐☐	Green Tea ☐☐☐	*Optional* (amount per day) Fiber _____ g **Calcium** _____ mg **Vitamin D** _____ IU			

BONUS TRACKER *(Record your blood sugar, track your medications, gauge your hunger, or make other notes here.)*

_____

_____

_____

_____

WORKOUT LOG

WORKOUTS	TIME	DURATION
	DAILY TOTAL EXERCISE TIME	

WORKOUT NOTES

How did you feel before? _____

_____

How did you feel after? _____

_____

Any obstacles? _____

_____

Major accomplishment? _____

_____

Other notes: _____

_____

PERSONAL NOTES

ENERGY LEVEL (circle one)
1 being "I'm so tired I can't get out of bed" and **10 being** "I could dance all night!"

1	2	3	4	5	6	7	8	9	10

SELF-ESTEEM/SELF-CONFIDENCE (circle one)
1 being "I can't do anything right" and **10 being** "I'm ready to change the world!"

1	2	3	4	5	6	7	8	9	10

FOOD LOG

	FOOD/DRINKS	TIME	CALORIES
Breakfast			
Lunch			
Snack			
Dinner			
Optional Snack			
	DAILY CALORIE TOTAL		

DAILY NUTRITION GOALS:	Grains/Starches	Fruits	Vegetables	Dairy	Healthy Fats	Lean Proteins
	☐☐☐☐☐☐	☐☐☐	☐☐☐☐☐	☐☐☐	☐☐☐☐	☐☐☐
	Water	**Green Tea**	*Optional* (amount per day)			
	☐☐☐☐☐	☐☐☐	Fiber _____ g **Calcium** _____ mg **Vitamin D** _____ IU			

BONUS TRACKER *(Record your blood sugar, track your medications, gauge your hunger, or make other notes here.)*

_____

_____

_____

_____

WORKOUT LOG

WORKOUTS	TIME	DURATION
	DAILY TOTAL EXERCISE TIME	

WORKOUT NOTES

How did you feel before? _____

_____

How did you feel after? _____

_____

Any obstacles? _____

_____

Major accomplishment? _____

_____

Other notes: _____

_____

PERSONAL NOTES

ENERGY LEVEL (circle one)
1 being "I'm so tired I can't get out of bed" and **10 being** "I could dance all night!"

1	2	3	4	5	6	7	8	9	10

SELF-ESTEEM/SELF-CONFIDENCE (circle one)
1 being "I can't do anything right" and **10 being** "I'm ready to change the world!"

1	2	3	4	5	6	7	8	9	10

FOOD LOG

	FOOD/DRINKS	TIME	CALORIES
Breakfast			
Lunch			
Snack			
Dinner			
Optional Snack			
		DAILY CALORIE TOTAL	

DAILY NUTRITION GOALS:	Grains/Starches □□□□□□	Fruits □□□	Vegetables □□□□□	Dairy □□□	Healthy Fats □□□□	Lean Proteins □□□
	Water □□□□□	Green Tea □□□	*Optional* (amount per day) Fiber _____g **Calcium** _____mg **Vitamin D** _____IU			

BONUS TRACKER *(Record your blood sugar, track your medications, gauge your hunger, or make other notes here.)*

_____

_____

_____

_____

WORKOUT LOG

WORKOUTS	TIME	DURATION
	DAILY TOTAL EXERCISE TIME	

WORKOUT NOTES

How did you feel before? _____

_____

How did you feel after? _____

_____

Any obstacles? _____

_____

Major accomplishment? _____

_____

Other notes: _____

_____

PERSONAL NOTES

ENERGY LEVEL (circle one)
1 being "I'm so tired I can't get out of bed" and **10 being** "I could dance all night!"

1	2	3	4	5	6	7	8	9	10

SELF-ESTEEM/SELF-CONFIDENCE (circle one)
1 being "I can't do anything right" and **10 being** "I'm ready to change the world!"

1	2	3	4	5	6	7	8	9	10

FOOD LOG

	FOOD/DRINKS	TIME	CALORIES
Breakfast			
Lunch			
Snack			
Dinner			
Optional Snack			
		DAILY CALORIE TOTAL	

DAILY NUTRITION GOALS:	Grains/Starches ☐☐☐☐☐☐	Fruits ☐☐☐	Vegetables ☐☐☐☐☐	Dairy ☐☐☐	Healthy Fats ☐☐☐☐	Lean Proteins ☐☐☐
	Water ☐☐☐☐☐	Green Tea ☐☐☐	Optional (amount per day) Fiber _____ g Calcium _____ mg Vitamin D _____ IU			

BONUS TRACKER *(Record your blood sugar, track your medications, gauge your hunger, or make other notes here.)*

_____

_____

_____

_____

WEEKLY MEASUREMENTS LOG

WEIGHT   _____
LBS

INCHES   _____   _____   _____
CHEST   LEFT THIGH   RIGHT THIGH

_____   _____   _____
WAIST   LEFT BICEPS   RIGHT BICEPS

_____
HIPS (at fullest part)

PERSONAL NOTES
ENERGY LEVEL (circle one)
1 being "I'm so tired I can't get out of bed" and **10 being** "I could dance all night!"

1	2	3	4	5	6	7	8	9	10

SELF ESTEEM/SELF-CONFIDENCE (circle one)
1 being "I can't do anything right" and **10 being** "I'm ready to change the world!"

1	2	3	4	5	6	7	8	9	10

Additional observations, challenges, notes:

_____

_____

_____

_____

_____

Additional observations, challenges, notes (cont'd):

_____

_____

_____

_____

_____

_____

_____

_____

_____

_____

_____

_____

_____

_____

_____

_____

_____

_____

_____

_____

_____

_____

_____

_____

_____

_____

WEEK 4
YOUR WORKOUT AT-A-GLANCE

DAY	ACTIVITY//WORKOUT	TOTAL
1	Basic Interval Walk II (45 min) // Lower-Body Strength Workout (15 min)	60 min
2	Toning Walk II (25 min)	25 min
3	Basic Interval Walk II (45 min)// Core Strength Workout (15 min)	60 min
4	Toning Walk II (25 min)	25 min
5	Basic Interval Walk II (45 min) // Lower-Body Strength Workout (15 min)	60 min
6	Long Walk IV (90 min) // Core Strength Workout (15 min)	105 min
7	Rest	

WHAT YOU'LL DO THIS WEEK

**3 x Basic Interval Walk II // 2 x Toning Walk II // 2 x Lower-Body Strength Workout
2 x Core Strength Workout // 1 x Long Walk IV**

Workout Summary

FOR DIRECTIONS, training tips, and advice on how to perform these exercises safely and at your personal fitness level, see chapter 5 of *Walk Off Weight*.

LOWER-BODY Routine
Do 12-15 reps of the following exercises:
>> **Cross Leg Swing**
>> **One-Leg Squat**
>> **Rear Kick**
>> **Reverse Lunge**
>> **Moving Squat**

CORE Routine
>> **Plank** *(Hold once for 1 minute)*
Do 12-15 reps of the following exercises:
>> **Tabletop Balance**
>> **Side Plank**
>> **Roll Down**
>> **Bicycle**

TECHNIQUE FOCUS: Quicker, Shorter Steps

One of the most common mistakes people make when they try to walk faster is that they take steps that are too long. The secret to speed is taking more, quicker steps, not excessively long ones. Think short as you step forward, keeping your stride more underneath and behind you.

A great way to push yourself to take quicker, shorter steps is to track your number of steps and then aim to increase it over the course of the program. You can simply count steps in your head for individual intervals or wear a pedometer to tally your step count for entire walks.

BASIC INTERVAL WALK II

TIME	ACTIVITY	INTENSITY	TIME	ACTIVITY	INTENSITY
0:00–5:00	Warm-Up (5 min)	3→5	22:30–23:00	Fast (30 sec)	7–8
5:00–6:00	Moderate (1 min)	5–6	23:00–24:00	Moderate (1 min)	5–6
6:00–6:30	Fast (30 sec)	7–8	24:00–24:30	Fast (30 sec)	7–8
6:30–7:30	Moderate (1 min)	5–6	24:30–25:30	Moderate (1 min)	5–6
7:30–8:00	Fast (30 sec)	7–8	25:30–26:00	Fast (30 sec)	7–8
8:00–9:00	Moderate (1 min)	5–6	26:00–27:00	Moderate (1 min)	5–6
9:00–9:30	Fast (30 sec)	7–8	27:00–27:30	Fast (30 sec)	7–8
9:30–10:30	Moderate (1 min)	5–6	27:30–28:30	Moderate (1 min)	5–6
10:30–11:00	Fast (30 sec)	7–8	28:30–29:00	Fast (30 sec)	7–8
11:00–12:00	Moderate (1 min)	5–6	29:00–30:00	Moderate (1 min)	5–6
12:00–12:30	Fast (30 sec)	7–8	30:00–30:30	Fast (30 sec)	7–8
12:30–13:30	Moderate (1 min)	5–6	30:30–31:30	Moderate (1 min)	5–6
13:30–14:00	Fast (30 sec)	7–8	31:30–32:00	Fast (30 sec)	7–8
14:00–15:00	Moderate (1 min)	5–6	32:00–33:00	Moderate (1 min)	5–6
15:00–15:30	Fast (30 sec)	7–8	33:00–33:30	Fast (30 sec)	7–8
15:30–16:30	Moderate (1 min)	5–6	33:30–34:30	Moderate (1 min)	5–6
16:30–17:00	Fast (30 sec)	7–8	34:30–35:00	Fast (30 sec)	7–8
17:00–18:00	Moderate (1 min)	5–6	35:00–36:00	Moderate (1 min)	5–6
18:00–18:30	Fast (30 sec)	7–8	36:00–36:30	Fast (30 sec)	7–8
18:30–19:30	Moderate (1 min)	5–6	36:30–37:30	Moderate (1 min)	5–6
19:30–20:00	Fast (30 sec)	7–8	37:30–38:00	Fast (30 sec)	7–8
20:00–21:00	Moderate (1 min)	5–6	38:00–39:00	Moderate (1 min)	5–6
21:00–21:30	Fast (30 sec)	7–8	39:00–39:30	Fast (30 sec)	7–8
21:30–22:30	Moderate (1 min)	5–6	39:30–40:30	Moderate (1 min)	5–6
			40:30–45:00	Cool-Down (4.5 min)	5→3

TONING WALK II

TIME	ACTIVITY	INTENSITY	TIME	ACTIVITY	INTENSITY
0:00–5:00	Warm-Up (5 min)	3→5	13:00–14:00	Row, left arm (1 min; 30 reps)	5–6
5:00–6:00	Pull-Down, right arm (1 min; 30 reps)	5–6	14:00–15:00	Brisk Walk (1 min)	6–7
6:00–7:00	Brisk Walk (1 min)	6–7	15:00–16:00	Overhead Press (1 min; 30 reps)	5–6
7:00–8:00	Pull-Down, left arm (1 min; 30 reps)	5–6	16:00–17:00	Brisk Walk (1 min)	6–7
8:00–9:00	Brisk Walk (1 min)	6–7	17:00–18:00	Front Pull (1 min; 30 reps)	5–6
9:00–10:00	Front Press (1 min; 30 reps)	5–6	18:00–19:00	Brisk Walk (1 min)	6–7
10:00–11:00	Brisk Walk (1 min)	6–7	19:00–20:00	Arm Pull (1 min; 30 reps)	5–6
11:00–12:00	Row, right arm (1 min; 30 reps)	5–6	20:00–21:00	Brisk Walk (1 min)	6–7
12:00–13:00	Brisk Walk (1 min)	6–7	21:00–25:00	Cool-Down (4 min)	5→3

LONG WALK IV

TIME	ACTIVITY	INTENSITY
0:00–5:00	Warm-Up (5 min)	3→5
5:00–85:00	Easy to Moderate Walk (80 min)	4–5
85:00–90:00	Cool-Down (5 min)	5→3

WORKOUT LOG

WORKOUTS	TIME	DURATION
	DAILY TOTAL EXERCISE TIME	

WORKOUT NOTES

How did you feel before? _____

_____

How did you feel after? _____

_____

Any obstacles? _____

_____

Major accomplishment? _____

_____

Other notes: _____

_____

PERSONAL NOTES

ENERGY LEVEL (circle one)
1 being "I'm so tired I can't get out of bed" and **10 being** "I could dance all night!"

1	2	3	4	5	6	7	8	9	10

SELF-ESTEEM/SELF-CONFIDENCE (circle one)
1 being "I can't do anything right" and **10 being** "I'm ready to change the world!"

1	2	3	4	5	6	7	8	9	10

FOOD LOG

	FOOD/DRINKS	TIME	CALORIES
Breakfast			
Lunch			
Snack			
Dinner			
Optional Snack			
	DAILY CALORIE TOTAL		

DAILY NUTRITION GOALS:	Grains/Starches ☐☐☐☐☐☐	Fruits ☐☐☐	Vegetables ☐☐☐☐☐	Dairy ☐☐☐	Healthy Fats ☐☐☐☐	Lean Proteins ☐☐☐
	Water ☐☐☐☐☐	Green Tea ☐☐☐	Optional (amount per day) Fiber _____ g Calcium _____ mg Vitamin D _____ IU			

BONUS TRACKER (*Record your blood sugar, track your medications, gauge your hunger, or make other notes here.*)

_____

_____

_____

_____

WORKOUT LOG

WORKOUTS	TIME	DURATION
	DAILY TOTAL EXERCISE TIME	

WORKOUT NOTES

How did you feel before? _____

_____

How did you feel after? _____

_____

Any obstacles? _____

_____

Major accomplishment? _____

_____

Other notes: _____

_____

PERSONAL NOTES

ENERGY LEVEL (circle one)
1 being "I'm so tired I can't get out of bed" and **10 being** "I could dance all night!"

1	2	3	4	5	6	7	8	9	10

SELF-ESTEEM/SELF-CONFIDENCE (circle one)
1 being "I can't do anything right" and **10 being** "I'm ready to change the world!"

1	2	3	4	5	6	7	8	9	10

FOOD LOG

	FOOD/DRINKS	TIME	CALORIES
Breakfast			
Lunch			
Snack			
Dinner			
Optional Snack			
		DAILY CALORIE TOTAL	

DAILY NUTRITION GOALS:	Grains/Starches ☐☐☐☐☐☐	Fruits ☐☐☐	Vegetables ☐☐☐☐☐	Dairy ☐☐☐	Healthy Fats ☐☐☐☐	Lean Proteins ☐☐☐
	Water ☐☐☐☐☐	Green Tea ☐☐☐	Optional (amount per day) Fiber _____ g Calcium _____ mg Vitamin D _____ IU			

BONUS TRACKER (*Record your blood sugar, track your medications, gauge your hunger, or make other notes here.*)

_____

_____

_____

_____

WORKOUT LOG

WORKOUTS	TIME	DURATION
	DAILY TOTAL EXERCISE TIME	

WORKOUT NOTES

How did you feel before? _____

_____

How did you feel after? _____

_____

Any obstacles? _____

_____

Major accomplishment? _____

_____

Other notes: _____

_____

PERSONAL NOTES

ENERGY LEVEL (circle one)
1 being "I'm so tired I can't get out of bed" and **10 being** "I could dance all night!"

1	2	3	4	5	6	7	8	9	10

SELF-ESTEEM/SELF-CONFIDENCE (circle one)
1 being "I can't do anything right" and **10 being** "I'm ready to change the world!"

1	2	3	4	5	6	7	8	9	10

FOOD LOG

	FOOD/DRINKS	TIME	CALORIES
Breakfast			
Lunch			
Snack			
Dinner			
Optional Snack			
		DAILY CALORIE TOTAL	

DAILY NUTRITION GOALS:	Grains/Starches ☐☐☐☐☐☐	Fruits ☐☐☐	Vegetables ☐☐☐☐☐	Dairy ☐☐☐	Healthy Fats ☐☐☐☐	Lean Proteins ☐☐☐
	Water ☐☐☐☐☐	Green Tea ☐☐☐	*Optional* (amount per day) Fiber _____ g Calcium _____ mg **Vitamin D** _____ IU			

BONUS TRACKER *(Record your blood sugar, track your medications, gauge your hunger, or make other notes here.)*

_____

_____

_____

_____

WORKOUT LOG

WORKOUTS	TIME	DURATION
	DAILY TOTAL EXERCISE TIME	

WORKOUT NOTES

How did you feel before? _____

_____

How did you feel after? _____

_____

Any obstacles? _____

_____

Major accomplishment? _____

_____

Other notes: _____

_____

PERSONAL NOTES

ENERGY LEVEL (circle one)
1 being "I'm so tired I can't get out of bed" and **10 being** "I could dance all night!"

1	2	3	4	5	6	7	8	9	10

SELF-ESTEEM/SELF-CONFIDENCE (circle one)
1 being "I can't do anything right" and **10 being** "I'm ready to change the world!"

1	2	3	4	5	6	7	8	9	10

FOOD LOG

	FOOD/DRINKS	TIME	CALORIES
Breakfast			
Lunch			
Snack			
Dinner			
Optional Snack			
		DAILY CALORIE TOTAL	

DAILY NUTRITION GOALS:	Grains/Starches	Fruits	Vegetables	Dairy	Healthy Fats	Lean Proteins
	☐☐☐☐☐☐	☐☐☐	☐☐☐☐☐	☐☐☐	☐☐☐☐	☐☐☐
	Water	Green Tea	Optional (amount per day)			
	☐☐☐☐☐	☐☐☐	Fiber _____ g Calcium _____ mg Vitamin D _____ IU			

BONUS TRACKER (*Record your blood sugar, track your medications, gauge your hunger, or make other notes here.*)

_____

_____

_____

_____

WORKOUT LOG

WORKOUTS	TIME	DURATION
	DAILY TOTAL EXERCISE TIME	

WORKOUT NOTES

How did you feel before? _____

_____

How did you feel after? _____

_____

Any obstacles? _____

_____

Major accomplishment? _____

_____

Other notes: _____

_____

PERSONAL NOTES

ENERGY LEVEL (circle one)
1 being "I'm so tired I can't get out of bed" and **10 being** "I could dance all night!"

1	2	3	4	5	6	7	8	9	10

SELF-ESTEEM/SELF-CONFIDENCE (circle one)
1 being "I can't do anything right" and **10 being** "I'm ready to change the world!"

1	2	3	4	5	6	7	8	9	10

FOOD LOG

	FOOD/DRINKS	TIME	CALORIES
Breakfast			
Lunch			
Snack			
Dinner			
Optional Snack			
		DAILY CALORIE TOTAL	

DAILY NUTRITION GOALS:	Grains/Starches	Fruits	Vegetables	Dairy	Healthy Fats	Lean Proteins
	☐☐☐☐☐☐	☐☐☐	☐☐☐☐☐	☐☐☐	☐☐☐☐	☐☐☐
	Water	Green Tea	Optional (amount per day)			
	☐☐☐☐☐	☐☐☐	Fiber _____ g Calcium _____ mg Vitamin D _____ IU			

BONUS TRACKER (*Record your blood sugar, track your medications, gauge your hunger, or make other notes here.*)

_____

_____

_____

_____

WORKOUT LOG

WORKOUTS	TIME	DURATION
	DAILY TOTAL EXERCISE TIME	

WORKOUT NOTES

How did you feel before? _____

_____

How did you feel after? _____

_____

Any obstacles? _____

_____

Major accomplishment? _____

_____

Other notes: _____

_____

PERSONAL NOTES

ENERGY LEVEL (circle one)
1 being "I'm so tired I can't get out of bed" and **10 being** "I could dance all night!"

1	2	3	4	5	6	7	8	9	10

SELF-ESTEEM/SELF-CONFIDENCE (circle one)
1 being "I can't do anything right" and **10 being** "I'm ready to change the world!"

1	2	3	4	5	6	7	8	9	10

FOOD LOG

	FOOD/DRINKS	TIME	CALORIES
Breakfast			
Lunch			
Snack			
Dinner			
Optional Snack			
		DAILY CALORIE TOTAL	

DAILY NUTRITION GOALS:	Grains/Starches ☐☐☐☐☐☐	Fruits ☐☐☐	Vegetables ☐☐☐☐☐	Dairy ☐☐☐	Healthy Fats ☐☐☐☐	Lean Proteins ☐☐☐
	Water ☐☐☐☐☐	Green Tea ☐☐☐	*Optional* (amount per day) Fiber _____g Calcium _____mg Vitamin D _____IU			

BONUS TRACKER (*Record your blood sugar, track your medications, gauge your hunger, or make other notes here.*)

_____

_____

_____

_____

WORKOUT LOG

WORKOUTS	TIME	DURATION
	DAILY TOTAL EXERCISE TIME	

WORKOUT NOTES

How did you feel before? _____

_____

How did you feel after? _____

_____

Any obstacles? _____

_____

Major accomplishment? _____

_____

Other notes: _____

_____

PERSONAL NOTES

ENERGY LEVEL (circle one)
1 being "I'm so tired I can't get out of bed" and **10 being** "I could dance all night!"

1	2	3	4	5	6	7	8	9	10

SELF-ESTEEM/SELF-CONFIDENCE (circle one)
1 being "I can't do anything right" and **10 being** "I'm ready to change the world!"

1	2	3	4	5	6	7	8	9	10

FOOD LOG

	FOOD/DRINKS	TIME	CALORIES
Breakfast			
Lunch			
Snack			
Dinner			
Optional Snack			
		DAILY CALORIE TOTAL	

DAILY NUTRITION GOALS:	Grains/Starches ☐☐☐☐☐☐	Fruits ☐☐☐	Vegetables ☐☐☐☐☐	Dairy ☐☐☐	Healthy Fats ☐☐☐☐	Lean Proteins ☐☐☐
	Water ☐☐☐☐☐	Green Tea ☐☐☐	*Optional* (amount per day) Fiber _____ g Calcium _____ mg **Vitamin D** _____ IU			

BONUS TRACKER *(Record your blood sugar, track your medications, gauge your hunger, or make other notes here.)*

_____

_____

_____

_____

WEEKLY MEASUREMENTS LOG

WEIGHT　　_____
LBS

INCHES　　_____　　_____　　_____
　　　　　　CHEST　　　LEFT THIGH　　RIGHT THIGH

　　　　　　_____　　_____　　_____
　　　　　　WAIST　　　LEFT BICEPS　　RIGHT BICEPS

　　　　　　_____
　　　　　　HIPS (at fullest part)

PERSONAL NOTES

ENERGY LEVEL (circle one)
1 being "I'm so tired I can't get out of bed" and **10 being** "I could dance all night!"

1	2	3	4	5	6	7	8	9	10

SELF-ESTEEM/SELF-CONFIDENCE (circle one)
1 being "I can't do anything right" and **10 being** "I'm ready to change the world!"

1	2	3	4	5	6	7	8	9	10

Additional observations, challenges, notes:

_____

_____

_____

_____

_____

Additional observations, challenges, notes (cont'd):

_____

_____

_____

_____

_____

_____

_____

_____

_____

_____

_____

_____

_____

_____

_____

_____

_____

_____

_____

_____

_____

_____

_____

_____

WEEK 5
YOUR WORKOUT AT-A-GLANCE

DAY	ACTIVITY//WORKOUT	TOTAL
1	Supercharged Interval Walk I (20 min)	20 min
2	Recovery Walk (20 min) // Total-Body Strength Workout (20 min)	40 min
3	Supercharged Interval Walk I (20 min)	20 min
4	Recovery Walk (20 min) // Total-Body Strength Workout (20 min)	40 min
5	Supercharged Interval Walk I (20 min)	20 min
6	Speed Walk (30 min) // Total-Body Strength Workout (20 min, optional)	about 50 min
7	Rest	

WHAT YOU'LL DO THIS WEEK

3 x Supercharged Interval Walk I
2 x Recovery Walk // 2 or 3 x Total-Body Strength Workout // 1 x Speed Walk

Workout Summary

FOR DIRECTIONS, training tips, and advice on how to perform these exercises safely and at your personal fitness level, see chapter 6 of *Walk Off Weight*.

TOTAL-BODY STRENGTH Workout
Do 8-10 reps of the following exercises:

>>**Balancing Deadlift with Arm Raise**
>>**Bridge with Press**
>>**Rotating Lunge**

>>**Row with Leg Swing**
>>**Crunch and Extend**
>>**Elevated Squat with Curl**

TECHNIQUE FOCUS: **Pull and Squeeze**

PULL Instead of letting momentum direct your arm swing, take control and put some power into it. Focus on the muscles in the middle of your upper back, pulling each arm back toward your hip.

SQUEEZE Each time your heel strikes the ground, your glutes should contract. Pay attention to it. Put your hand on your butt and feel it. Really squeeze. Use these powerful muscles to pull your body over your front leg and propel you forward. Walking isn't just about pushing your body forward with your back foot. By using both legs, the back one to push you forward and the front one to pull you forward, you'll have a more powerful, faster stride.

SUPERCHARGED INTERVAL WALK I

YOU'LL BE DOING 15-second high-intensity speed bursts. The intervals are super-short so that you can really push yourself. Then, you'll recover for 30 seconds.

TIME	ACTIVITY	INTENSITY	TIME	ACTIVITY	INTENSITY
0:00–5:00	Warm-Up (5 min)	3➔5	10:45–11:15	Easy to Mod (30 sec)	4–6
5:00–6:00	Moderate (1 min)	5–6	11:15–11:30	Very Fast (15 sec)	8–9
6:00–6:15	Very Fast (15 sec)	8–9	11:30–12:00	Easy to Mod (30 sec)	4–6
6:15–6:45	Easy to Mod (30 sec)	4–6	12:00–12:15	Very Fast (15 sec)	8–9
6:45–7:00	Very Fast (15 sec)	8–9	12:15–12:45	Easy to Mod (30 sec)	4–6
7:00–7:30	Easy to Mod (30 sec)	4–6	12:45–13:00	Very Fast (15 sec)	8–9
7:30–7:45	Very Fast (15 sec)	8–9	13:00–13:30	Easy to Mod (30 sec)	4–6
7:45–8:15	Easy to Mod (30 sec)	4–6	13:30–13:45	Very Fast (15 sec)	8–9
8:15–8:30	Very Fast (15 sec)	8–9	13:45–14:15	Easy to Mod (30 sec)	4–6
8:30–9:00	Easy to Mod (30 sec)	4–6	14:15–14:30	Very Fast (15 sec)	8–9
9:00–9:15	Very Fast (15 sec)	8–9	14:30–15:00	Easy to Mod (30 sec)	4–6
9:15–9:45	Easy to Mod (30 sec)	4–6	15:00–15:15	Very Fast (15 sec)	8–9
9:45–10:00	Very Fast (15 sec)	8–9	15:15–15:45	Easy to Mod (30 sec)	4–6
10:00–10:30	Easy to Mod (30 sec)	4–6	15:45–16:00	Very Fast (15 sec)	8–9
10:30–10:45	Very Fast (15 sec)	8–9	16:00–16:30	Easy to Mod (30 sec)	4–6
			16:30–20:00	Cool-Down (3.5 min)	5➔3

RECOVERY WALK

THE PURPOSE OF THIS WALK is to get your body moving a little following the previous day's high-intensity workout. You may also boost your fat burn and curb your appetite by doing cardio and strength training on the same day.

TIME	ACTIVITY	INTENSITY
0:00–3:00	Warm-Up (3 min)	3➔5
3:00–18:00	Moderate Walk (15 min)	5–6
18:00–20:00	Cool-Down (2 min)	5➔3

SPEED WALK

THE FOCUS OF THIS WALK is to push yourself to go faster. Map out a 1-mile route. Do your warm-up and cool-down separate from the 1-mile route so in total you'll be walking a little over 1 mile. During the 1-mile route, go at a pace that you feel you can maintain for the entire distance. You should be breathing heavy (about a 6 to 8 intensity level), but not panting. Make note of your time on the logs provided.

ACTIVITY	INTENSITY
Warm-Up (5 min)	3➔5
Very Fast Walk (times will vary)	6–8
Cool-Down (5 min)	5➔3

WORKOUT LOG

WORKOUTS	TIME	DURATION
	DAILY TOTAL EXERCISE TIME	

WORKOUT NOTES

How did you feel before? _____

_____

How did you feel after? _____

_____

Any obstacles? _____

_____

Major accomplishment? _____

_____

Other notes: _____

_____

PERSONAL NOTES

ENERGY LEVEL (circle one)
1 being "I'm so tired I can't get out of bed" and **10 being** "I could dance all night!"

1	2	3	4	5	6	7	8	9	10

SELF-ESTEEM/SELF-CONFIDENCE (circle one)
1 being "I can't do anything right" and **10 being** "I'm ready to change the world!"

1	2	3	4	5	6	7	8	9	10

FOOD LOG

	FOOD/DRINKS	TIME	CALORIES
Breakfast			
Lunch			
Snack			
Dinner			
Optional Snack			
		DAILY CALORIE TOTAL	

DAILY NUTRITION GOALS:	Grains/Starches ☐☐☐☐☐☐	Fruits ☐☐☐	Vegetables ☐☐☐☐☐	Dairy ☐☐☐	Healthy Fats ☐☐☐☐	Lean Proteins ☐☐☐
	Water ☐☐☐☐☐	Green Tea ☐☐☐	*Optional* (amount per day) Fiber _____ g Calcium _____ mg **Vitamin D** _____ IU			

BONUS TRACKER (*Record your blood sugar, track your medications, gauge your hunger, or make other notes here.*)

_____

_____

_____

_____

WORKOUT LOG

WORKOUTS	TIME	DURATION
	DAILY TOTAL EXERCISE TIME	

WORKOUT NOTES

How did you feel before? _____

_____

How did you feel after? _____

_____

Any obstacles? _____

_____

Major accomplishment? _____

_____

Other notes: _____

_____

PERSONAL NOTES

ENERGY LEVEL (circle one)
1 being "I'm so tired I can't get out of bed" and **10 being** "I could dance all night!"

1	2	3	4	5	6	7	8	9	10

SELF-ESTEEM/SELF-CONFIDENCE (circle one)
1 being "I can't do anything right" and **10 being** "I'm ready to change the world!"

1	2	3	4	5	6	7	8	9	10

FOOD LOG

	FOOD/DRINKS	TIME	CALORIES
Breakfast			
Lunch			
Snack			
Dinner			
Optional Snack			
		DAILY CALORIE TOTAL	

DAILY NUTRITION GOALS:	Grains/Starches ☐☐☐☐☐☐	Fruits ☐☐☐	Vegetables ☐☐☐☐☐	Dairy ☐☐☐	Healthy Fats ☐☐☐☐	Lean Proteins ☐☐☐
	Water ☐☐☐☐☐	Green Tea ☐☐☐	Optional (amount per day) Fiber _____ g Calcium _____ mg Vitamin D _____ IU			

BONUS TRACKER (*Record your blood sugar, track your medications, gauge your hunger, or make other notes here.*)

_____

_____

_____

_____

WORKOUT LOG

WORKOUTS	TIME	DURATION
	DAILY TOTAL EXERCISE TIME	

WORKOUT NOTES

How did you feel before? _____

_____

How did you feel after? _____

_____

Any obstacles? _____

_____

Major accomplishment? _____

_____

Other notes: _____

_____

PERSONAL NOTES

ENERGY LEVEL (circle one)
1 being "I'm so tired I can't get out of bed" and **10 being** "I could dance all night!"

1	2	3	4	5	6	7	8	9	10

SELF-ESTEEM/SELF-CONFIDENCE (circle one)
1 being "I can't do anything right" and **10 being** "I'm ready to change the world!"

1	2	3	4	5	6	7	8	9	10

FOOD LOG

	FOOD/DRINKS	TIME	CALORIES
Breakfast			
Lunch			
Snack			
Dinner			
Optional Snack			
		DAILY CALORIE TOTAL	

DAILY NUTRITION GOALS:	Grains/Starches	Fruits	Vegetables	Dairy	Healthy Fats	Lean Proteins
	☐☐☐☐☐☐	☐☐☐	☐☐☐☐☐	☐☐☐	☐☐☐☐	☐☐☐
	Water	Green Tea	Optional (amount per day)			
	☐☐☐☐☐	☐☐☐	Fiber _____ g Calcium _____ mg Vitamin D _____ IU			

BONUS TRACKER *(Record your blood sugar, track your medications, gauge your hunger, or make other notes here.)*

_____

_____

_____

_____

WORKOUT LOG

WORKOUTS	TIME	DURATION
	DAILY TOTAL EXERCISE TIME	

WORKOUT NOTES

How did you feel before? _____

_____

How did you feel after? _____

_____

Any obstacles? _____

_____

Major accomplishment? _____

_____

Other notes: _____

_____

PERSONAL NOTES

ENERGY LEVEL (circle one)
1 being "I'm so tired I can't get out of bed" and **10 being** "I could dance all night!"

1	2	3	4	5	6	7	8	9	10

SELF-ESTEEM/SELF-CONFIDENCE (circle one)
1 being "I can't do anything right" and **10 being** "I'm ready to change the world!"

1	2	3	4	5	6	7	8	9	10

FOOD LOG

	FOOD/DRINKS	TIME	CALORIES
Breakfast			
Lunch			
Snack			
Dinner			
Optional Snack			
		DAILY CALORIE TOTAL	

DAILY NUTRITION GOALS:	Grains/Starches ☐☐☐☐☐☐	Fruits ☐☐☐	Vegetables ☐☐☐☐☐	Dairy ☐☐☐	Healthy Fats ☐☐☐☐	Lean Proteins ☐☐☐
	Water ☐☐☐☐☐	Green Tea ☐☐☐	*Optional* (amount per day) Fiber _____ g Calcium _____ mg Vitamin D _____ IU			

BONUS TRACKER *(Record your blood sugar, track your medications, gauge your hunger, or make other notes here.)*

_____

_____

_____

_____

WORKOUT LOG

WORKOUTS	TIME	DURATION
	DAILY TOTAL EXERCISE TIME	

WORKOUT NOTES

How did you feel before? _____

_____

How did you feel after? _____

_____

Any obstacles? _____

_____

Major accomplishment? _____

_____

Other notes: _____

_____

PERSONAL NOTES

ENERGY LEVEL (circle one)
1 being "I'm so tired I can't get out of bed" and **10 being** "I could dance all night!"

1	2	3	4	5	6	7	8	9	10

SELF-ESTEEM/SELF-CONFIDENCE (circle one)
1 being "I can't do anything right" and **10 being** "I'm ready to change the world!"

1	2	3	4	5	6	7	8	9	10

PHASE 2 WALK OFF WEIGHT

FOOD LOG

	FOOD/DRINKS	TIME	CALORIES
Breakfast			
Lunch			
Snack			
Dinner			
Optional Snack			
		DAILY CALORIE TOTAL	

DAILY NUTRITION GOALS:	Grains/Starches	Fruits	Vegetables	Dairy	Healthy Fats	Lean Proteins
	☐☐☐☐☐☐	☐☐☐	☐☐☐☐☐	☐☐☐	☐☐☐☐	☐☐☐
	Water	Green Tea	*Optional* (amount per day)			
	☐☐☐☐☐	☐☐☐	Fiber _____ g **Calcium** _____ mg **Vitamin D** _____ IU			

BONUS TRACKER *(Record your blood sugar, track your medications, gauge your hunger, or make other notes here.)*

_____

_____

_____

_____

WORKOUT LOG

WORKOUTS	TIME	DURATION
	DAILY TOTAL EXERCISE TIME	

WORKOUT NOTES

How did you feel before? _____

_____

How did you feel after? _____

_____

Any obstacles? _____

_____

Major accomplishment? _____

_____

Other notes: _____

_____

PERSONAL NOTES

ENERGY LEVEL (circle one)
1 being "I'm so tired I can't get out of bed" and **10 being** "I could dance all night!"

1	2	3	4	5	6	7	8	9	10

SELF-ESTEEM/SELF-CONFIDENCE (circle one)
1 being "I can't do anything right" and **10 being** "I'm ready to change the world!"

1	2	3	4	5	6	7	8	9	10

PHASE 2 WALK OFF WEIGHT

FOOD LOG

	FOOD/DRINKS	TIME	CALORIES
Breakfast			
Lunch			
Snack			
Dinner			
Optional Snack			
		DAILY CALORIE TOTAL	

DAILY NUTRITION GOALS:

Grains/Starches ☐☐☐☐☐☐ Fruits ☐☐☐ Vegetables ☐☐☐☐☐ Dairy ☐☐☐ Healthy Fats ☐☐☐☐ Lean Proteins ☐☐☐

Water ☐☐☐☐☐ Green Tea ☐☐☐ *Optional* (amount per day) Fiber _____ g **Calcium** _____ mg **Vitamin D** _____ IU

BONUS TRACKER *(Record your blood sugar, track your medications, gauge your hunger, or make other notes here.)*

_____

_____

_____

_____

99

WORKOUT LOG

WORKOUTS	TIME	DURATION
	DAILY TOTAL EXERCISE TIME	

WORKOUT NOTES

How did you feel before? _____

_____

How did you feel after? _____

_____

Any obstacles? _____

_____

Major accomplishment? _____

_____

Other notes: _____

_____

PERSONAL NOTES

ENERGY LEVEL (circle one)
1 being "I'm so tired I can't get out of bed" and **10 being** "I could dance all night!"

1	2	3	4	5	6	7	8	9	10

SELF-ESTEEM/SELF-CONFIDENCE (circle one)
1 being "I can't do anything right" and **10 being** "I'm ready to change the world!"

1	2	3	4	5	6	7	8	9	10

FOOD LOG

	FOOD/DRINKS	TIME	CALORIES
Breakfast			
Lunch			
Snack			
Dinner			
Optional Snack			
		DAILY CALORIE TOTAL	

DAILY NUTRITION GOALS:	Grains/Starches ☐☐☐☐☐☐	Fruits ☐☐☐	Vegetables ☐☐☐☐☐	Dairy ☐☐☐	Healthy Fats ☐☐☐☐	Lean Proteins ☐☐☐
	Water ☐☐☐☐☐	Green Tea ☐☐☐	*Optional* (amount per day) Fiber _____ g	Calcium _____ mg	Vitamin D _____ IU	

BONUS TRACKER *(Record your blood sugar, track your medications, gauge your hunger, or make other notes here.)*

_____

_____

_____

_____

WEEKLY MEASUREMENTS LOG

WEIGHT   _____
LBS

INCHES   _____   _____   _____
CHEST   LEFT THIGH   RIGHT THIGH

_____   _____   _____
WAIST   LEFT BICEPS   RIGHT BICEPS

_____
HIPS (at fullest part)

PERSONAL NOTES

ENERGY LEVEL (circle one)
1 being "I'm so tired I can't get out of bed" and **10 being** "I could dance all night!"

1	2	3	4	5	6	7	8	9	10

SELF-ESTEEM/SELF-CONFIDENCE (circle one)
1 being "I can't do anything right" and **10 being** "I'm ready to change the world!"

1	2	3	4	5	6	7	8	9	10

Additional observations, challenges, notes:

_____

_____

_____

_____

_____

Additional observations, challenges, notes (cont'd):

_____

_____

_____

_____

_____

_____

_____

_____

_____

_____

_____

_____

_____

_____

_____

_____

_____

_____

_____

_____

_____

_____

WEEK 6
YOUR WORKOUT AT-A-GLANCE

DAY	ACTIVITY//WORKOUT	TOTAL
1	Supercharged Interval Walk I (20 min)	20 min
2	Recovery Walk (20 min) // Total-Body Strength Workout (20 min)	40 min
3	Supercharged Interval I Walk (20 min)	20 min
4	Recovery Walk (20 min) // Total-Body Strength Workout (20 min)	40 min
5	Supercharged Interval I Walk (20 min)	20 min
6	Speed Walk (30 min) // Total-Body Strength Workout (20 min, optional)	about 50 min
7	Rest	

IIIIIIIIIIIIIIIIIIIIIIIIIIIIIIIIIIIIIIIIIIIIIIIIIIIIIIIIIIIIIIIIIIIIIIIIIIIIIIIIIIIIIIIIIIIIIIIIIIII

WHAT YOU'LL DO THIS WEEK

3 x Supercharged Interval Walk I
2 x Recovery Walk // 3 x Total-Body Strength Workout // 1 x Speed Walk

IIIIIIIIIIIIIIIIIIIIIIIIIIIIIIIIIIIIIIIIIIIIIIIIIIIIIIIIIIIIIIIIIIIIIIIIIIIIIIIIIIIIIIIIIIIIIIIIIIII

Workout Summary

FOR DIRECTIONS, training tips, and advice on how to perform these exercises safely and at your personal fitness level, see chapter 6 of *Walk Off Weight*.

TOTAL-BODY STRENGTH Workout
Do 10-12 reps of the following exercises:

>>**Balancing Deadlift with Arm Raise**
>>**Bridge with Press**
>>**Rotating Lunge**

>>**Row with Leg Swing**
>>**Crunch and Extend**
>>**Elevated Squat with Curl**

TECHNIQUE FOCUS: Swivel Hips

The hip action you want is forward and back, not side to side. Imagine that your legs start up around your navel and that your hip is an extension of your leg. To loosen up your hips so they move more freely, walk like a model, crossing your legs over each other as you step, for a few minutes during your warm-up.

SUPERCHARGED INTERVAL WALK I

TIME	ACTIVITY	INTENSITY
0:00–5:00	Warm-Up (5 min)	3→5
5:00–6:00	Moderate (1 min)	5–6
6:00–6:15	Very Fast (15 sec)	8–9
6:15–6:45	Easy to Mod (30 sec)	4–6
6:45–7:00	Very Fast (15 sec)	8–9
7:00–7:30	Easy to Mod (30 sec)	4–6
7:30–7:45	Very Fast (15 sec)	8–9
7:45–8:15	Easy to Mod (30 sec)	4–6
8:15–8:30	Very Fast (15 sec)	8–9
8:30–9:00	Easy to Mod (30 sec)	4–6
9:00–9:15	Very Fast (15 sec)	8–9
9:15–9:45	Easy to Mod (30 sec)	4–6
9:45–10:00	Very Fast (15 sec)	8–9
10:00–10:30	Easy to Mod (30 sec)	4–6
10:30–10:45	Very Fast (15 sec)	8–9

TIME	ACTIVITY	INTENSITY
10:45–11:15	Easy to Mod (30 sec)	4–6
11:15–11:30	Very Fast (15 sec)	8–9
11:30–12:00	Easy to Mod (30 sec)	4–6
12:00–12:15	Very Fast (15 sec)	8–9
12:15–12:45	Easy to Mod (30 sec)	4–6
12:45–13:00	Very Fast (15 sec)	8–9
13:00–13:30	Easy to Mod (30 sec)	4–6
13:30–13:45	Very Fast (15 sec)	8–9
13:45–14:15	Easy to Mod (30 sec)	4–6
14:15–14:30	Very Fast (15 sec)	8–9
14:30–15:00	Easy to Mod (30 sec)	4–6
15:00–15:15	Very Fast (15 sec)	8–9
15:15–15:45	Easy to Mod (30 sec)	4–6
15:45–16:00	Very Fast (15 sec)	8–9
16:00–16:30	Easy to Mod (30 sec)	4–6
16:30–20:00	Cool-Down (3.5 min)	3→5

RECOVERY WALK

TIME	ACTIVITY	INTENSITY
0:00–3:00	Warm-Up (3 min)	3→5
3:00–18:00	Moderate Walk (15 min)	5–6
18:00–20:00	Cool-Down (2 min)	5→3

SPEED WALK

ACTIVITY	INTENSITY
Warm-Up (5 min)	3→5
Very Fast Walk (times will vary)	6–8
Cool-Down (5 min)	5→3

WORKOUT LOG

WORKOUTS	TIME	DURATION
	DAILY TOTAL EXERCISE TIME	

WORKOUT NOTES

How did you feel before? _____

_____

How did you feel after? _____

_____

Any obstacles? _____

_____

Major accomplishment? _____

_____

Other notes: _____

_____

PERSONAL NOTES

ENERGY LEVEL (circle one)
1 being "I'm so tired I can't get out of bed" and **10 being** "I could dance all night!"

1	2	3	4	5	6	7	8	9	10

SELF-ESTEEM/SELF-CONFIDENCE (circle one)
1 being "I can't do anything right" and **10 being** "I'm ready to change the world!"

1	2	3	4	5	6	7	8	9	10

FOOD LOG

	FOOD/DRINKS	TIME	CALORIES
Breakfast			
Lunch			
Snack			
Dinner			
Optional Snack			
		DAILY CALORIE TOTAL	

DAILY NUTRITION GOALS:	Grains/Starches ☐☐☐☐☐☐	Fruits ☐☐☐	Vegetables ☐☐☐☐☐	Dairy ☐☐☐	Healthy Fats ☐☐☐☐	Lean Proteins ☐☐☐
	Water ☐☐☐☐☐	Green Tea ☐☐☐	*Optional* (amount per day) Fiber _____ g Calcium _____ mg **Vitamin D** _____ IU			

BONUS TRACKER (*Record your blood sugar, track your medications, gauge your hunger, or make other notes here.*)

_____

_____

_____

_____

WORKOUT LOG

WORKOUTS	TIME	DURATION
	DAILY TOTAL EXERCISE TIME	

WORKOUT NOTES

How did you feel before? _____

_____

How did you feel after? _____

_____

Any obstacles? _____

_____

Major accomplishment? _____

_____

Other notes: _____

_____

PERSONAL NOTES

ENERGY LEVEL (circle one)
1 being "I'm so tired I can't get out of bed" and **10 being** "I could dance all night!"

1	2	3	4	5	6	7	8	9	10

SELF-ESTEEM/SELF-CONFIDENCE (circle one)
1 being "I can't do anything right" and **10 being** "I'm ready to change the world!"

1	2	3	4	5	6	7	8	9	10

FOOD LOG

	FOOD/DRINKS	TIME	CALORIES
Breakfast			
Lunch			
Snack			
Dinner			
Optional Snack			
		DAILY CALORIE TOTAL	

DAILY NUTRITION GOALS:	Grains/Starches ☐☐☐☐☐☐	Fruits ☐☐☐	Vegetables ☐☐☐☐☐	Dairy ☐☐☐	Healthy Fats ☐☐☐☐	Lean Proteins ☐☐☐
	Water ☐☐☐☐☐	Green Tea ☐☐☐	*Optional* (amount per day) Fiber _____g Calcium _____mg **Vitamin D** _____IU			

BONUS TRACKER *(Record your blood sugar, track your medications, gauge your hunger, or make other notes here.)*

_____

_____

_____

_____

WORKOUT LOG

WORKOUTS	TIME	DURATION
	DAILY TOTAL EXERCISE TIME	

WORKOUT NOTES

How did you feel before? _____

_____

How did you feel after? _____

_____

Any obstacles? _____

_____

Major accomplishment? _____

_____

Other notes: _____

_____

PERSONAL NOTES

ENERGY LEVEL (circle one)
1 being "I'm so tired I can't get out of bed" and **10 being** "I could dance all night!"

1	2	3	4	5	6	7	8	9	10

SELF-ESTEEM/SELF-CONFIDENCE (circle one)
1 being "I can't do anything right" and **10 being** "I'm ready to change the world!"

1	2	3	4	5	6	7	8	9	10

FOOD LOG

	FOOD/DRINKS	TIME	CALORIES
Breakfast			
Lunch			
Snack			
Dinner			
Optional Snack			
	DAILY CALORIE TOTAL		

DAILY NUTRITION GOALS:	Grains/Starches	Fruits	Vegetables	Dairy	Healthy Fats	Lean Proteins
	☐☐☐☐☐☐	☐☐☐	☐☐☐☐☐	☐☐☐	☐☐☐☐	☐☐☐
	Water	**Green Tea**	*Optional* (amount per day)			
	☐☐☐☐☐	☐☐☐	Fiber _____ g **Calcium** _____ mg **Vitamin D** _____ IU			

BONUS TRACKER *(Record your blood sugar, track your medications, gauge your hunger, or make other notes here.)*

_____

_____

_____

_____

WORKOUT LOG

WORKOUTS	TIME	DURATION
	DAILY TOTAL EXERCISE TIME	

WORKOUT NOTES

How did you feel before? _____

_____

How did you feel after? _____

_____

Any obstacles? _____

_____

Major accomplishment? _____

_____

Other notes: _____

_____

PERSONAL NOTES

ENERGY LEVEL (circle one)
1 being "I'm so tired I can't get out of bed" and **10 being** "I could dance all night!"

1	2	3	4	5	6	7	8	9	10

SELF-ESTEEM/SELF-CONFIDENCE (circle one)
1 being "I can't do anything right" and **10 being** "I'm ready to change the world!"

1	2	3	4	5	6	7	8	9	10

FOOD LOG

	FOOD/DRINKS	TIME	CALORIES
Breakfast			
Lunch			
Snack			
Dinner			
Optional Snack			
	DAILY CALORIE TOTAL		

DAILY NUTRITION GOALS:	Grains/Starches ☐☐☐☐☐☐	Fruits ☐☐☐	Vegetables ☐☐☐☐☐	Dairy ☐☐☐	Healthy Fats ☐☐☐☐	Lean Proteins ☐☐☐
	Water ☐☐☐☐☐	Green Tea ☐☐☐	*Optional* (amount per day) Fiber _____g Calcium _____mg **Vitamin D** _____IU			

BONUS TRACKER *(Record your blood sugar, track your medications, gauge your hunger, or make other notes here.)*

_____

_____

_____

_____

113

WORKOUT LOG

WORKOUTS	TIME	DURATION
	DAILY TOTAL EXERCISE TIME	

WORKOUT NOTES

How did you feel before? _____

_____

How did you feel after? _____

_____

Any obstacles? _____

_____

Major accomplishment? _____

_____

Other notes: _____

_____

PERSONAL NOTES

ENERGY LEVEL (circle one)
1 being "I'm so tired I can't get out of bed" and **10 being** "I could dance all night!"

1	2	3	4	5	6	7	8	9	10

SELF-ESTEEM/SELF-CONFIDENCE (circle one)
1 being "I can't do anything right" and **10 being** "I'm ready to change the world!"

1	2	3	4	5	6	7	8	9	10

FOOD LOG

	FOOD/DRINKS	TIME	CALORIES
Breakfast			
Lunch			
Snack			
Dinner			
Optional Snack			
	DAILY CALORIE TOTAL		

DAILY NUTRITION GOALS:	Grains/Starches ☐☐☐☐☐☐	Fruits ☐☐☐	Vegetables ☐☐☐☐☐	Dairy ☐☐☐	Healthy Fats ☐☐☐☐	Lean Proteins ☐☐☐
	Water ☐☐☐☐☐	Green Tea ☐☐☐	Optional (amount per day) Fiber _____ g Calcium _____ mg Vitamin D _____ IU			

BONUS TRACKER (*Record your blood sugar, track your medications, gauge your hunger, or make other notes here.*)

_____

_____

_____

_____

WORKOUT LOG

WORKOUTS	TIME	DURATION
	DAILY TOTAL EXERCISE TIME	

WORKOUT NOTES

How did you feel before? _____

_____

How did you feel after? _____

_____

Any obstacles? _____

_____

Major accomplishment? _____

_____

Other notes: _____

_____

PERSONAL NOTES

ENERGY LEVEL (circle one)
1 being "I'm so tired I can't get out of bed" and **10 being** "I could dance all night!"

1	2	3	4	5	6	7	8	9	10

SELF-ESTEEM/SELF-CONFIDENCE (circle one)
1 being "I can't do anything right" and **10 being** "I'm ready to change the world!"

1	2	3	4	5	6	7	8	9	10

FOOD LOG

	FOOD/DRINKS	TIME	CALORIES
Breakfast			
Lunch			
Snack			
Dinner			
Optional Snack			
	DAILY CALORIE TOTAL		

DAILY NUTRITION GOALS:	Grains/Starches ☐☐☐☐☐☐	Fruits ☐☐☐	Vegetables ☐☐☐☐☐	Dairy ☐☐☐	Healthy Fats ☐☐☐☐	Lean Proteins ☐☐☐
	Water ☐☐☐☐☐	Green Tea ☐☐☐	*Optional* (amount per day) Fiber _____ g Calcium _____ mg Vitamin D _____ IU			

BONUS TRACKER (*Record your blood sugar, track your medications, gauge your hunger, or make other notes here.*)

_____

_____

_____

_____

WORKOUT LOG

WORKOUTS	TIME	DURATION
	DAILY TOTAL EXERCISE TIME	

WORKOUT NOTES

How did you feel before? _____

_____

How did you feel after? _____

_____

Any obstacles? _____

_____

Major accomplishment? _____

_____

Other notes: _____

_____

PERSONAL NOTES

ENERGY LEVEL (circle one)
1 being "I'm so tired I can't get out of bed" and **10 being** "I could dance all night!"

1	2	3	4	5	6	7	8	9	10

SELF-ESTEEM/SELF-CONFIDENCE (circle one)
1 being "I can't do anything right" and **10 being** "I'm ready to change the world!"

1	2	3	4	5	6	7	8	9	10

FOOD LOG

	FOOD/DRINKS	TIME	CALORIES
Breakfast			
Lunch			
Snack			
Dinner			
Optional Snack			
		DAILY CALORIE TOTAL	

DAILY NUTRITION GOALS:	Grains/Starches ☐☐☐☐☐☐	Fruits ☐☐☐	Vegetables ☐☐☐☐☐	Dairy ☐☐☐	Healthy Fats ☐☐☐☐	Lean Proteins ☐☐☐
	Water ☐☐☐☐☐	Green Tea ☐☐☐	Optional (amount per day) Fiber _____ g Calcium _____ mg Vitamin D _____ IU			

BONUS TRACKER (*Record your blood sugar, track your medications, gauge your hunger, or make other notes here.*)

_____

_____

_____

_____

WEEKLY MEASUREMENTS LOG

WEIGHT _____
LBS

INCHES _____   _____   _____
CHEST   LEFT THIGH   RIGHT THIGH

_____   _____   _____
WAIST   LEFT BICEPS   RIGHT BICEPS

_____
HIPS (at fullest part)

PERSONAL NOTES
ENERGY LEVEL (circle one)
1 being "I'm so tired I can't get out of bed" and **10 being** "I could dance all night!"

| 1 | 2 | 3 | 4 | 5 | 6 | 7 | 8 | 9 | 10 |

SELF-ESTEEM/SELF-CONFIDENCE (circle one)
1 being "I can't do anything right" and **10 being** "I'm ready to change the world!"

| 1 | 2 | 3 | 4 | 5 | 6 | 7 | 8 | 9 | 10 |

Additional observations, challenges, notes:

_____

_____

_____

_____

_____

Additional observations, challenges, notes (cont'd):

_____

_____

_____

_____

_____

_____

_____

_____

_____

_____

_____

_____

_____

_____

_____

_____

_____

_____

_____

_____

_____

_____

_____

_____

_____

_____

WEEK 7
YOUR WORKOUT AT-A-GLANCE

DAY	ACTIVITY//WORKOUT	TOTAL
1	Supercharged Interval Walk II (30 min)	30 min
2	Recovery Walk (25 min) // Total-Body Strength Workout (20 min)	40 min
3	Supercharged Interval Walk II (30 min)	30 min
4	Recovery Walk (25 min) // Total-Body Strength Workout (20 min)	40 min
5	Supercharged Interval Walk II (30 min)	30 min
6	Speed Walk (30 min) // Total-Body Strength Workout (20 min, optional)	<50 min
7	Rest	

‖‖

WHAT YOU'LL DO THIS WEEK

3 x Supercharged Interval Walk II
2 x Recovery Walk // 2 or 3 x Total-Body Strength Workout // 1 x Speed Walk

‖‖

Workout Summary

FOR DIRECTIONS, training tips, and advice on how to perform these exercises safely and at your personal fitness level, see chapter 6 of *Walk Off Weight*.

TOTAL-BODY STRENGTH Workout
Do 15–17 reps of the following exercises:

>>**Balancing Deadlift with Arm Raise**   >>**Row with Leg Swing**
>>**Bridge with Press**   >>**Crunch and Extend**
>>**Rotating Lunge**   >>**Elevated Squat with Curl**

TECHNIQUE FOCUS: Put It All Together

You have everything you need, so give it your all these last 2 weeks!

SUPERCHARGED INTERVAL WALK II

TIME	ACTIVITY	INTENSITY	TIME	ACTIVITY	INTENSITY
0:00–5:00	Warm-Up (5 min)	3➜5	15:15–15:45	Easy to Mod (30 sec)	4–6
5:00–6:00	Moderate (1 min)	5–6	15:45–16:00	Very Fast (15 sec)	8–9
6:00–6:15	Very Fast (15 sec)	8–9	16:00–16:30	Easy to Mod (30 sec)	4–6
6:15–6:45	Easy to Mod (30 sec)	4–6	16:30–16:45	Very Fast (15 sec)	8–9
6:45–7:00	Very Fast (15 sec)	8–9	16:45–17:15	Easy to Mod (30 sec)	4–6
7:00–7:30	Easy to Mod (30 sec)	4–6	17:15–17:30	Very Fast (15 sec)	8–9
7:30–7:45	Very Fast (15 sec)	8–9	17:30–18:00	Easy to Mod (30 sec)	4–6
7:45–8:15	Easy to Mod (30 sec)	4–6	18:00–18:15	Very Fast (15 sec)	8–9
8:15–8:30	Very Fast (15 sec)	8–9	18:15–18:45	Easy to Mod (30 sec)	4–6
8:30–9:00	Easy to Mod (30 sec)	4–6	18:45–19:00	Very Fast (15 sec)	8–9
9:00–9:15	Very Fast (15 sec)	8–9	19:00–19:30	Easy to Mod (30 sec)	4–6
9:15–9:45	Easy to Mod (30 sec)	4–6	19:30–19:45	Very Fast (15 sec)	8–9
9:45–10:00	Very Fast (15 sec)	8–9	19:45–20:15	Easy to Mod (30 sec)	4–6
10:00–10:30	Easy to Mod (30 sec)	4–6	20:15–20:30	Very Fast (15 sec)	8–9
10:30–10:45	Very Fast (15 sec)	8–9	20:30–21:00	Easy to Mod (30 sec)	4–6
10:45–11:15	Easy to Mod (30 sec)	4–6	21:00–21:15	Very Fast (15 sec)	8–9
11:15–11:30	Very Fast (15 sec)	8–9	21:15–21:45	Easy to Mod (30 sec)	4–6
11:30–12:00	Easy to Mod (30 sec)	4–6	21:45–22:00	Very Fast (15 sec)	8–9
12:00–12:15	Very Fast (15 sec)	8–9	22:00–22:30	Easy to Mod (30 sec)	4–6
12:15–12:45	Easy to Mod (30 sec)	4–6	22:30–22:45	Very Fast (15 sec)	8–9
12:45–13:00	Very Fast (15 sec)	8–9	22:45–23:15	Easy to Mod (30 sec)	4–6
13:00–13:30	Easy to Mod (30 sec)	4–6	23:15–23:30	Very Fast (15 sec)	8–9
13:30–13:45	Very Fast (15 sec)	8–9	23:30–24:00	Easy to Mod (30 sec)	4–6
13:45–14:15	Easy to Mod (30 sec)	4–6	24:00–24:15	Very Fast (15 sec)	8–9
14:15–14:30	Very Fast (15 sec)	8–9	24:15–24:45	Easy to Mod (30 sec)	4–6
14:30–15:00	Easy to Mod (30 sec)	4–6	24:45–25:00	Very Fast (15 sec)	8–9
15:00–15:15	Very Fast (15 sec)	8–9	25:00–25:30	Easy to Mod (30 sec)	4–6
			25:30–30:00	Cool-Down (4.5 min)	5➜3

RECOVERY WALK

TIME	ACTIVITY	INTENSITY
0:00–3:00	Warm-Up (3 min)	3➜5
3:00–18:00	Moderate Walk (20 min)	5–6
18:00–20:00	Cool-Down (2 min)	5➜3

SPEED WALK

ACTIVITY	INTENSITY
Warm-Up (5 min)	3➜5
Very Fast Walk (times will vary)	6–8
Cool-Down (5 min)	5➜3

WORKOUT LOG

WORKOUTS	TIME	DURATION
	DAILY TOTAL EXERCISE TIME	

WORKOUT NOTES

How did you feel before? _____

_____

How did you feel after? _____

_____

Any obstacles? _____

_____

Major accomplishment? _____

_____

Other notes: _____

_____

PERSONAL NOTES

ENERGY LEVEL (circle one)
1 being "I'm so tired I can't get out of bed" and **10 being** "I could dance all night!"

1	2	3	4	5	6	7	8	9	10

SELF-ESTEEM/SELF-CONFIDENCE (circle one)
1 being "I can't do anything right" and **10 being** "I'm ready to change the world!"

1	2	3	4	5	6	7	8	9	10

FOOD LOG

	FOOD/DRINKS	TIME	CALORIES
Breakfast			
Lunch			
Snack			
Dinner			
Optional Snack			
		DAILY CALORIE TOTAL	

DAILY NUTRITION GOALS:	Grains/Starches	Fruits	Vegetables	Dairy	Healthy Fats	Lean Proteins
	☐☐☐☐☐☐	☐☐☐	☐☐☐☐☐	☐☐☐	☐☐☐☐	☐☐☐
	Water	Green Tea	Optional (amount per day)			
	☐☐☐☐☐	☐☐☐	Fiber ____ g Calcium ____ mg Vitamin D ____ IU			

BONUS TRACKER (*Record your blood sugar, track your medications, gauge your hunger, or make other notes here.*)

_____

_____

_____

_____

125

WORKOUT LOG

WORKOUTS	TIME	DURATION
	DAILY TOTAL EXERCISE TIME	

WORKOUT NOTES

How did you feel before? _____

_____

How did you feel after? _____

_____

Any obstacles? _____

_____

Major accomplishment? _____

_____

Other notes: _____

_____

PERSONAL NOTES

ENERGY LEVEL (circle one)
1 being "I'm so tired I can't get out of bed" and **10 being** "I could dance all night!"

1	2	3	4	5	6	7	8	9	10

SELF-ESTEEM/SELF-CONFIDENCE (circle one)
1 being "I can't do anything right" and **10 being** "I'm ready to change the world!"

1	2	3	4	5	6	7	8	9	10

FOOD LOG

	FOOD/DRINKS	TIME	CALORIES
Breakfast			
Lunch			
Snack			
Dinner			
Optional Snack			
		DAILY CALORIE TOTAL	

DAILY NUTRITION GOALS:	Grains/Starches ☐☐☐☐☐☐	Fruits ☐☐☐	Vegetables ☐☐☐☐☐	Dairy ☐☐☐	Healthy Fats ☐☐☐☐	Lean Proteins ☐☐☐
	Water ☐☐☐☐☐	Green Tea ☐☐☐	Optional (amount per day) Fiber _____ g Calcium _____ mg Vitamin D _____ IU			

BONUS TRACKER (*Record your blood sugar, track your medications, gauge your hunger, or make other notes here.*)

_____

_____

_____

_____

WORKOUT LOG

WORKOUTS	TIME	DURATION
	DAILY TOTAL EXERCISE TIME	

WORKOUT NOTES

How did you feel before? _____

_____

How did you feel after? _____

_____

Any obstacles? _____

_____

Major accomplishment? _____

_____

Other notes: _____

_____

PERSONAL NOTES

ENERGY LEVEL (circle one)
1 being "I'm so tired I can't get out of bed" and **10 being** "I could dance all night!"

1	2	3	4	5	6	7	8	9	10

SELF-ESTEEM/SELF-CONFIDENCE (circle one)
1 being "I can't do anything right" and **10 being** "I'm ready to change the world!"

1	2	3	4	5	6	7	8	9	10

FOOD LOG

	FOOD/DRINKS	TIME	CALORIES
Breakfast			
Lunch			
Snack			
Dinner			
Optional Snack			
	DAILY CALORIE TOTAL		

DAILY NUTRITION GOALS:	Grains/Starches	Fruits	Vegetables	Dairy	Healthy Fats	Lean Proteins
	☐☐☐☐☐☐	☐☐☐	☐☐☐☐☐	☐☐☐	☐☐☐☐	☐☐☐
	Water	**Green Tea**	*Optional* (amount per day)			
	☐☐☐☐☐	☐☐☐	**Fiber** _____ g **Calcium** _____ mg **Vitamin D** _____ IU			

BONUS TRACKER *(Record your blood sugar, track your medications, gauge your hunger, or make other notes here.)*

_____

_____

_____

_____

WORKOUT LOG

WORKOUTS	TIME	DURATION
	DAILY TOTAL EXERCISE TIME	

WORKOUT NOTES

How did you feel before? _____

_____

How did you feel after? _____

_____

Any obstacles? _____

_____

Major accomplishment? _____

_____

Other notes: _____

_____

PERSONAL NOTES

ENERGY LEVEL (circle one)
1 being "I'm so tired I can't get out of bed" and **10 being** "I could dance all night!"

1	2	3	4	5	6	7	8	9	10

SELF-ESTEEM/SELF-CONFIDENCE (circle one)
1 being "I can't do anything right" and **10 being** "I'm ready to change the world!"

1	2	3	4	5	6	7	8	9	10

FOOD LOG

	FOOD/DRINKS	TIME	CALORIES
Breakfast			
Lunch			
Snack			
Dinner			
Optional Snack			
	DAILY CALORIE TOTAL		

DAILY NUTRITION GOALS:	Grains/Starches	Fruits	Vegetables	Dairy	Healthy Fats	Lean Proteins
	☐☐☐☐☐☐	☐☐☐	☐☐☐☐☐	☐☐☐	☐☐☐☐	☐☐☐
	Water	Green Tea	Optional (amount per day)			
	☐☐☐☐☐	☐☐☐	Fiber _____ g **Calcium** _____ mg **Vitamin D** _____ IU			

BONUS TRACKER *(Record your blood sugar, track your medications, gauge your hunger, or make other notes here.)*

_____

_____

_____

_____

WORKOUT LOG

WORKOUTS	TIME	DURATION
	DAILY TOTAL EXERCISE TIME	

WORKOUT NOTES

How did you feel before? _____

_____

How did you feel after? _____

_____

Any obstacles? _____

_____

Major accomplishment? _____

_____

Other notes: _____

_____

PERSONAL NOTES

ENERGY LEVEL (circle one)
1 being "I'm so tired I can't get out of bed" and **10 being** "I could dance all night!"

1	2	3	4	5	6	7	8	9	10

SELF-ESTEEM/SELF-CONFIDENCE (circle one)
1 being "I can't do anything right" and **10 being** "I'm ready to change the world!"

1	2	3	4	5	6	7	8	9	10

FOOD LOG

	FOOD/DRINKS	TIME	CALORIES
Breakfast			
Lunch			
Snack			
Dinner			
Optional Snack			
	DAILY CALORIE TOTAL		

DAILY NUTRITION GOALS:

Grains/Starches ☐☐☐☐☐☐ Fruits ☐☐☐ Vegetables ☐☐☐☐☐ Dairy ☐☐☐ Healthy Fats ☐☐☐☐ Lean Proteins ☐☐☐

Water ☐☐☐☐☐ Green Tea ☐☐☐ *Optional* (amount per day) Fiber ____ g **Calcium** ____ mg **Vitamin D** ____ IU

BONUS TRACKER (*Record your blood sugar, track your medications, gauge your hunger, or make other notes here.*)

_____

_____

_____

_____

133

WORKOUT LOG

WORKOUTS	TIME	DURATION
	DAILY TOTAL EXERCISE TIME	

WORKOUT NOTES

How did you feel before? _____

_____

How did you feel after? _____

_____

Any obstacles? _____

_____

Major accomplishment? _____

_____

Other notes: _____

_____

PERSONAL NOTES

ENERGY LEVEL (circle one)
1 being "I'm so tired I can't get out of bed" and **10 being** "I could dance all night!"

1	2	3	4	5	6	7	8	9	10

SELF-ESTEEM/SELF-CONFIDENCE (circle one)
1 being "I can't do anything right" and **10 being** "I'm ready to change the world!"

1	2	3	4	5	6	7	8	9	10

FOOD LOG

	FOOD/DRINKS	TIME	CALORIES
Breakfast			
Lunch			
Snack			
Dinner			
Optional Snack			
	DAILY CALORIE TOTAL		

DAILY NUTRITION GOALS:	Grains/Starches	Fruits	Vegetables	Dairy	Healthy Fats	Lean Proteins
	☐☐☐☐☐☐	☐☐☐	☐☐☐☐☐	☐☐☐	☐☐☐☐	☐☐☐
	Water	Green Tea	Optional (amount per day)			
	☐☐☐☐☐	☐☐☐	Fiber _____ g Calcium _____ mg **Vitamin D** _____ IU			

BONUS TRACKER (Record your blood sugar, track your medications, gauge your hunger, or make other notes here.)

_____

_____

_____

_____

WORKOUT LOG

WORKOUTS	TIME	DURATION
	DAILY TOTAL EXERCISE TIME	

WORKOUT NOTES

How did you feel before? _____

_____

How did you feel after? _____

_____

Any obstacles? _____

_____

Major accomplishment? _____

_____

Other notes: _____

_____

PERSONAL NOTES

ENERGY LEVEL (circle one)
1 being "I'm so tired I can't get out of bed" and **10 being** "I could dance all night!"

1	2	3	4	5	6	7	8	9	10

SELF-ESTEEM/SELF-CONFIDENCE (circle one)
1 being "I can't do anything right" and **10 being** "I'm ready to change the world!"

1	2	3	4	5	6	7	8	9	10

FOOD LOG

	FOOD/DRINKS	TIME	CALORIES
Breakfast			
Lunch			
Snack			
Dinner			
Optional Snack			
		DAILY CALORIE TOTAL	

DAILY NUTRITION GOALS:	Grains/Starches ☐☐☐☐☐☐	Fruits ☐☐☐	Vegetables ☐☐☐☐☐	Dairy ☐☐☐	Healthy Fats ☐☐☐☐	Lean Proteins ☐☐☐
	Water ☐☐☐☐☐	Green Tea ☐☐☐	*Optional* (amount per day) Fiber _____ g Calcium _____ mg Vitamin D _____ IU			

BONUS TRACKER *(Record your blood sugar, track your medications, gauge your hunger, or make other notes here.)*

_____

_____

_____

_____

DATE/TIME _____

WEEKLY MEASUREMENTS LOG

WEIGHT _____
LBS

INCHES

_____	_____	_____
CHEST	LEFT THIGH	RIGHT THIGH

_____	_____	_____
WAIST	LEFT BICEPS	RIGHT BICEPS

_____
HIPS (at fullest part)

PERSONAL NOTES

ENERGY LEVEL (circle one)
1 being "I'm so tired I can't get out of bed" and **10 being** "I could dance all night!"

1	2	3	4	5	6	7	8	9	10

SELF-ESTEEM/SELF-CONFIDENCE (circle one)
1 being "I can't do anything right" and **10 being** "I'm ready to change the world!"

1	2	3	4	5	6	7	8	9	10

Additional observations, challenges, notes:

_____

_____

_____

_____

_____

Additional observations, challenges, notes (cont'd):

_____

_____

_____

_____

_____

_____

_____

_____

_____

_____

_____

_____

_____

_____

_____

_____

_____

_____

_____

_____

_____

_____

_____

_____

WEEK 8
YOUR WORKOUT AT-A-GLANCE

DAY	ACTIVITY//WORKOUT	TOTAL
1	Supercharged Interval Walk II (30 min)	30 min
2	Recovery Walk (25 min) // Total-Body Strength Workout (20 min)	40 min
3	Supercharged Interval Walk II (30 min)	30 min
4	Recovery Walk (25 min) // Total-Body Strength Workout (20 min)	40 min
5	Supercharged Interval Walk II (30 min)	30 min
6	Speed Walk (30 min) // Total-Body Strength Workout (20 min, optional)	<50 min
7	Rest	

||||||||||||||||||||||||||||||||||||||||||||||||||||||||||||||||||||||||||||||||||||||||||||||||||||||||||

WHAT YOU'LL DO THIS WEEK

3 x Supercharged Interval Walk II
2 x Recovery Walk // 2 x or 3 x Total-Body Strength Workout // 1 x Speed Walk

||||||||||||||||||||||||||||||||||||||||||||||||||||||||||||||||||||||||||||||||||||||||||||||||||||||||||

Workout Summary

FOR DIRECTIONS, training tips, and advice on how to perform these exercises safely and at your personal fitness level, see chapter 6 of *Walk Off Weight*.

TOTAL-BODY STRENGTH Workout
Do 18-20 reps of the following exercises:

>>**Balancing Deadlift with Arm Raise**
>>**Bridge with Press**
>>**Rotating Lunge**

>>**Row with Leg Swing**
>>**Crunch and Extend**
>>**Elevated Squat with Curl**

TECHNIQUE FOCUS: Keep It Up

Eyes up, arms bent, fast steps! You know what to do, so get out there and do it!

SUPERCHARGED INTERVAL WALK II

TIME	ACTIVITY	INTENSITY	TIME	ACTIVITY	INTENSITY
0:00–5:00	Warm-Up (5 min)	3→5	15:15–15:45	Easy to Mod (30 sec)	4–6
5:00–6:00	Moderate (1 min)	5–6	15:45–16:00	Very Fast (15 sec)	8–9
6:00–6:15	Very Fast (15 sec)	8–9	16:00–16:30	Easy to Mod (30 sec)	4–6
6:15–6:45	Easy to Mod (30 sec)	4–6	16:30–16:45	Very Fast (15 sec)	8–9
6:45–7:00	Very Fast (15 sec)	8–9	16:45–17:15	Easy to Mod (30 sec)	4–6
7:00–7:30	Easy to Mod (30 sec)	4–6	17:15–17:30	Very Fast (15 sec)	8–9
7:30–7:45	Very Fast (15 sec)	8–9	17:30–18:00	Easy to Mod (30 sec)	4–6
7:45–8:15	Easy to Mod (30 sec)	4–6	18:00–18:15	Very Fast (15 sec)	8–9
8:15–8:30	Very Fast (15 sec)	8–9	18:15–18:45	Easy to Mod (30 sec)	4–6
8:30–9:00	Easy to Mod (30 sec)	4–6	18:45–19:00	Very Fast (15 sec)	8–9
9:00–9:15	Very Fast (15 sec)	8–9	19:00–19:30	Easy to Mod (30 sec)	4–6
9:15–9:45	Easy to Mod (30 sec)	4–6	19:30–19:45	Very Fast (15 sec)	8–9
9:45–10:00	Very Fast (15 sec)	8–9	19:45–20:15	Easy to Mod (30 sec)	4–6
10:00–10:30	Easy to Mod (30 sec)	4–6	20:15–20:30	Very Fast (15 sec)	8–9
10:30–10:45	Very Fast (15 sec)	8–9	20:30–21:00	Easy to Mod (30 sec)	4–6
10:45–11:15	Easy to Mod (30 sec)	4–6	21:00–21:15	Very Fast (15 sec)	8–9
11:15–11:30	Very Fast (15 sec)	8–9	21:15–21:45	Easy to Mod (30 sec)	4–6
11:30–12:00	Easy to Mod (30 sec)	4–6	21:45–22:00	Very Fast (15 sec)	8–9
12:00–12:15	Very Fast (15 sec)	8–9	22:00–22:30	Easy to Mod (30 sec)	4–6
12:15–12:45	Easy to Mod (30 sec)	4–6	22:30–22:45	Very Fast (15 sec)	8–9
12:45–13:00	Very Fast (15 sec)	8–9	22:45–23:15	Easy to Mod (30 sec)	4–6
13:00–13:30	Easy to Mod (30 sec)	4–6	23:15–23:30	Very Fast (15 sec)	8–9
13:30–13:45	Very Fast (15 sec)	8–9	23:30–24:00	Easy to Mod (30 sec)	4–6
13:45–14:15	Easy to Mod (30 sec)	4–6	24:00–24:15	Very Fast (15 sec)	8–9
14:15–14:30	Very Fast (15 sec)	8–9	24:15–24:45	Easy to Mod (30 sec)	4–6
14:30–15:00	Easy to Mod (30 sec)	4–6	24:45–25:00	Very Fast (15 sec)	8–9
15:00–15:15	Very Fast (15 sec)	8–9	25:00–25:30	Easy to Mod (30 sec)	4–6
			25:30–30:00	Cool-Down (4.5 min)	5→3

RECOVERY WALK

TIME	ACTIVITY	INTENSITY
0:00–3:00	Warm-Up (3 min)	3→5
3:00–18:00	Moderate Walk (20 min)	5–6
18:00–20:00	Cool-Down (2 min)	5→3

SPEED WALK

ACTIVITY	INTENSITY
Warm-Up (5 min)	3→5
Very Fast Walk (times will vary)	6–8
Cool-Down (5 min)	5→3

WORKOUT LOG

WORKOUTS	TIME	DURATION
	DAILY TOTAL EXERCISE TIME	

WORKOUT NOTES

How did you feel before? _____

_____

How did you feel after? _____

_____

Any obstacles? _____

_____

Major accomplishment? _____

_____

Other notes: _____

_____

PERSONAL NOTES

ENERGY LEVEL (circle one)
1 being "I'm so tired I can't get out of bed" and **10 being** "I could dance all night!"

1	2	3	4	5	6	7	8	9	10

SELF-ESTEEM/SELF-CONFIDENCE (circle one)
1 being "I can't do anything right" and **10 being** "I'm ready to change the world!"

1	2	3	4	5	6	7	8	9	10

FOOD LOG

	FOOD/DRINKS	TIME	CALORIES
Breakfast			
Lunch			
Snack			
Dinner			
Optional Snack			
		DAILY CALORIE TOTAL	

DAILY NUTRITION GOALS:	Grains/Starches	Fruits	Vegetables	Dairy	Healthy Fats	Lean Proteins
	☐☐☐☐☐☐	☐☐☐	☐☐☐☐☐	☐☐☐	☐☐☐☐	☐☐☐
	Water	Green Tea	*Optional* (amount per day)			
	☐☐☐☐☐	☐☐☐	Fiber _____ g Calcium _____ mg Vitamin D _____ IU			

BONUS TRACKER *(Record your blood sugar, track your medications, gauge your hunger, or make other notes here.)*

_____

_____

_____

_____

WORKOUT LOG

WORKOUTS	TIME	DURATION
	DAILY TOTAL EXERCISE TIME	

WORKOUT NOTES

How did you feel before? _____

_____

How did you feel after? _____

_____

Any obstacles? _____

_____

Major accomplishment? _____

_____

Other notes: _____

_____

PERSONAL NOTES

ENERGY LEVEL (circle one)
1 being "I'm so tired I can't get out of bed" and **10 being** "I could dance all night!"

| 1 | 2 | 3 | 4 | 5 | 6 | 7 | 8 | 9 | 10 |

SELF-ESTEEM/SELF-CONFIDENCE (circle one)
1 being "I can't do anything right" and **10 being** "I'm ready to change the world!"

| 1 | 2 | 3 | 4 | 5 | 6 | 7 | 8 | 9 | 10 |

FOOD LOG

	FOOD/DRINKS	TIME	CALORIES
Breakfast			
Lunch			
Snack			
Dinner			
Optional Snack			
		DAILY CALORIE TOTAL	

DAILY NUTRITION GOALS:	Grains/Starches	Fruits	Vegetables	Dairy	Healthy Fats	Lean Proteins
	☐☐☐☐☐☐	☐☐☐	☐☐☐☐☐	☐☐☐	☐☐☐☐	☐☐☐
	Water	Green Tea	Optional (amount per day)			
	☐☐☐☐☐	☐☐☐	Fiber _____ g Calcium _____ mg Vitamin D _____ IU			

BONUS TRACKER (Record your blood sugar, track your medications, gauge your hunger, or make other notes here.)

_____

_____

_____

_____

WORKOUT LOG

WORKOUTS	TIME	DURATION
	DAILY TOTAL EXERCISE TIME	

WORKOUT NOTES

How did you feel before? _____

_____

How did you feel after? _____

_____

Any obstacles? _____

_____

Major accomplishment? _____

_____

Other notes: _____

_____

PERSONAL NOTES

ENERGY LEVEL (circle one)
1 being "I'm so tired I can't get out of bed" and **10 being** "I could dance all night!"

| 1 | 2 | 3 | 4 | 5 | 6 | 7 | 8 | 9 | 10 |

SELF-ESTEEM/SELF-CONFIDENCE (circle one)
1 being "I can't do anything right" and **10 being** "I'm ready to change the world!"

| 1 | 2 | 3 | 4 | 5 | 6 | 7 | 8 | 9 | 10 |

FOOD LOG

	FOOD/DRINKS	TIME	CALORIES
Breakfast			
Lunch			
Snack			
Dinner			
Optional Snack			
		DAILY CALORIE TOTAL	

DAILY NUTRITION GOALS:

Grains/Starches ☐☐☐☐☐☐ Fruits ☐☐☐ Vegetables ☐☐☐☐☐ Dairy ☐☐☐ Healthy Fats ☐☐☐☐ Lean Proteins ☐☐☐

Water ☐☐☐☐☐ Green Tea ☐☐☐ *Optional* (amount per day) Fiber ____g Calcium ____mg Vitamin D ____IU

BONUS TRACKER (*Record your blood sugar, track your medications, gauge your hunger, or make other notes here.*)

_____

_____

_____

_____

147

WORKOUT LOG

WORKOUTS	TIME	DURATION
	DAILY TOTAL EXERCISE TIME	

WORKOUT NOTES

How did you feel before? _____

_____

How did you feel after? _____

_____

Any obstacles? _____

_____

Major accomplishment? _____

_____

Other notes: _____

_____

PERSONAL NOTES

ENERGY LEVEL (circle one)
1 being "I'm so tired I can't get out of bed" and **10 being** "I could dance all night!"

| 1 | 2 | 3 | 4 | 5 | 6 | 7 | 8 | 9 | 10 |

SELF-ESTEEM/SELF-CONFIDENCE (circle one)
1 being "I can't do anything right" and **10 being** "I'm ready to change the world!"

| 1 | 2 | 3 | 4 | 5 | 6 | 7 | 8 | 9 | 10 |

FOOD LOG

	FOOD/DRINKS	TIME	CALORIES
Breakfast			
Lunch			
Snack			
Dinner			
Optional Snack			
	DAILY CALORIE TOTAL		

DAILY NUTRITION GOALS:	Grains/Starches ☐☐☐☐☐☐	Fruits ☐☐☐	Vegetables ☐☐☐☐☐	Dairy ☐☐☐	Healthy Fats ☐☐☐☐	Lean Proteins ☐☐☐
	Water ☐☐☐☐☐	Green Tea ☐☐☐	Optional (amount per day) Fiber _____ g Calcium _____ mg Vitamin D _____ IU			

BONUS TRACKER (*Record your blood sugar, track your medications, gauge your hunger, or make other notes here.*)

_____

_____

_____

_____

149

WORKOUT LOG

WORKOUTS	TIME	DURATION
	DAILY TOTAL EXERCISE TIME	

WORKOUT NOTES

How did you feel before? _____

_____

How did you feel after? _____

_____

Any obstacles? _____

_____

Major accomplishment? _____

_____

Other notes: _____

_____

PERSONAL NOTES

ENERGY LEVEL (circle one)
1 being "I'm so tired I can't get out of bed" and **10 being** "I could dance all night!"

1	2	3	4	5	6	7	8	9	10

SELF-ESTEEM/SELF-CONFIDENCE (circle one)
1 being "I can't do anything right" and **10 being** "I'm ready to change the world!"

1	2	3	4	5	6	7	8	9	10

FOOD LOG

	FOOD/DRINKS	TIME	CALORIES
Breakfast			
Lunch			
Snack			
Dinner			
Optional Snack			
		DAILY CALORIE TOTAL	

DAILY NUTRITION GOALS:	Grains/Starches ☐☐☐☐☐☐	Fruits ☐☐☐	Vegetables ☐☐☐☐☐	Dairy ☐☐☐	Healthy Fats ☐☐☐☐	Lean Proteins ☐☐☐
	Water ☐☐☐☐☐	Green Tea ☐☐☐	*Optional* (amount per day) Fiber _____ g Calcium _____ mg **Vitamin D** _____ IU			

BONUS TRACKER (*Record your blood sugar, track your medications, gauge your hunger, or make other notes here.*)

_____

_____

_____

_____

WORKOUT LOG

WORKOUTS	TIME	DURATION
	DAILY TOTAL EXERCISE TIME	

WORKOUT NOTES

How did you feel before? _____

_____

How did you feel after? _____

_____

Any obstacles? _____

_____

Major accomplishment? _____

_____

Other notes: _____

_____

PERSONAL NOTES

ENERGY LEVEL (circle one)
1 being "I'm so tired I can't get out of bed" and **10 being** "I could dance all night!"

1	2	3	4	5	6	7	8	9	10

SELF-ESTEEM/SELF-CONFIDENCE (circle one)
1 being "I can't do anything right" and **10 being** "I'm ready to change the world!"

1	2	3	4	5	6	7	8	9	10

FOOD LOG

	FOOD/DRINKS	TIME	CALORIES
Breakfast			
Lunch			
Snack			
Dinner			
Optional Snack			
		DAILY CALORIE TOTAL	

DAILY NUTRITION GOALS:	Grains/Starches	Fruits	Vegetables	Dairy	Healthy Fats	Lean Proteins
	☐☐☐☐☐☐	☐☐☐	☐☐☐☐☐	☐☐☐	☐☐☐☐	☐☐☐
	Water	Green Tea	Optional (amount per day)			
	☐☐☐☐☐	☐☐☐	Fiber _____ g Calcium _____ mg **Vitamin D** _____ IU			

BONUS TRACKER (Record your blood sugar, track your medications, gauge your hunger, or make other notes here.)

_____

_____

_____

_____

WORKOUT LOG

WORKOUTS	TIME	DURATION
	DAILY TOTAL EXERCISE TIME	

WORKOUT NOTES

How did you feel before? _____

_____

How did you feel after? _____

_____

Any obstacles? _____

_____

Major accomplishment? _____

_____

Other notes: _____

_____

PERSONAL NOTES

ENERGY LEVEL (circle one)
1 being "I'm so tired I can't get out of bed" and **10 being** "I could dance all night!"

1	2	3	4	5	6	7	8	9	10

SELF-ESTEEM/SELF-CONFIDENCE (circle one)
1 being "I can't do anything right" and **10 being** "I'm ready to change the world!"

1	2	3	4	5	6	7	8	9	10

FOOD LOG

	FOOD/DRINKS	TIME	CALORIES
Breakfast			
Lunch			
Snack			
Dinner			
Optional Snack			
		DAILY CALORIE TOTAL	

DAILY NUTRITION GOALS:	Grains/Starches ☐☐☐☐☐☐	Fruits ☐☐☐	Vegetables ☐☐☐☐☐	Dairy ☐☐☐	Healthy Fats ☐☐☐☐	Lean Proteins ☐☐☐
	Water ☐☐☐☐☐	Green Tea ☐☐☐	Optional (amount per day) Fiber ____g Calcium ____mg Vitamin D ____IU			

BONUS TRACKER *(Record your blood sugar, track your medications, gauge your hunger, or make other notes here.)*

_____

_____

_____

_____

WEEKLY MEASUREMENTS LOG

WEIGHT _____
LBS

INCHES

_____   _____   _____
CHEST   LEFT THIGH   RIGHT THIGH

_____   _____   _____
WAIST   LEFT BICEPS   RIGHT BICEPS

_____
HIPS (at fullest part)

PERSONAL NOTES

ENERGY LEVEL (circle one)
1 being "I'm so tired I can't get out of bed" and **10 being** "I could dance all night!"

1	2	3	4	5	6	7	8	9	10

SELF-ESTEEM/SELF-CONFIDENCE (circle one)
1 being "I can't do anything right" and **10 being** "I'm ready to change the world!"

1	2	3	4	5	6	7	8	9	10

Additional observations, challenges, notes:

_____

_____

_____

_____

_____

Additional observations, challenges, notes (cont'd):

_____

_____

_____

_____

_____

_____

_____

_____

_____

_____

_____

_____

_____

_____

_____

_____

_____

_____

_____

_____

_____

_____

_____

_____

_____

_____

_____

_____

BEYOND 8 WEEKS
Don't Stop Now!

Whether you're looking to lose some more pounds, get firmer, or just maintain the results you've already achieved, you can continue using the WOW program to meet your goals. **The next 8 weeks of journal pages each start with a blank "Workout at-a-Glance" chart that you can fill in to customize your weekly exercise routine.** And remember that no matter which type of workouts you're doing or what your goals are, the WOW meal plan and eating guidelines will keep you satisfied and provide all the nutrients you need.

TO LOSE MORE WEIGHT

>> **Do the Basic "Lose More" Plan (formerly Week 4) for 4 to 6 weeks.**
>> **Then do the Supercharged "Lose More" Plan (formerly Week 8) for the next 4 to 6 weeks.**
>> **Or alternate these plans weekly for 10 to 12 weeks.**

Continue with one or both of these cycles until you reach your goal weight, then follow the WOW Maintenance Plan on page 160 of this journal. During that time, try some of the advanced toning workouts and alternate interval workouts in chapter 9 of *Walk Off Weight* for variety and faster results. Remember, challenging your body in new ways will keep the results coming and help you avoid a plateau.

LOSE MORE PLAN WORKOUT SCHEDULE

DAY	BASIC	TOTAL	SUPERCHARGED	TOTAL
1	Basic Interval Walk II, (45 min) // Lower-Body Strength Workout (15 min)	60 min	Supercharged Interval Walk II (30 min)	30 min
2	Toning Walk II (25 min)	25 min	Recovery Walk (25 min) // Total-Body Strength Workout (20 min)	45 min
3	Basic Interval Walk II (45 min) // Core Strength Workout (15 min)	60 min	Supercharged Interval Walk II (30 min)	30 min
4	Toning Walk II (25 min)	25 min	Recovery Walk (25 min) // Total-Body Strength Workout (20 min)	45 min
5	Basic Interval Walk II (45 min) // Lower-Body Strength Workout (15 min)	60 min	Supercharged Interval Walk II (30 min)	30 min
6	Long Walk (1–2 hours) // Core Strength Workout (15 min)	75–135 min	Speed Walk (30) min // Total-Body Strength Workout (20 min)	<50 min
7	Rest		Rest	

TO GET FIRMER

This plan is similar to the "To Lose More Weight" option, but you'll be progressing your toning workout.

>> **Do the Basic "Get Firmer" Plan (formerly Week 4) for 4 to 6 weeks, doing either the "Make It Harder" variations for the toning workouts or trying the alternate routines in chapter 9 of *Walk Off Weight* (you can reduce the number of reps to work up to these harder moves).**

>> **Then do the Supercharged "Get Firmer" Plan (formerly Week 8) for the next 4 to 6 weeks, doing either the "Make It Harder" variations for the toning workouts or trying the alternate routines in chapter 9 of *Walk Off Weight* (you can reduce the number of reps to work up to these harder moves).**

Continue this cycle until you are as toned as you want to be, and then follow the WOW Maintenance Plan on page 160 of this journal. During that time, try some of the alternate interval workouts in chapter 9 of *Walk Off Weight* for variety and faster results. Remember, challenging your body in new ways will keep the results coming and help you avoid a plateau.

GET FIRMER PLAN WORKOUT SCHEDULE

DAY	BASIC	TOTAL	SUPERCHARGED	TOTAL
1	Basic Interval Walk II (45 min) // Lower-Body Strength Workout (15 min)	60 min	Supercharged Interval Walk II (30 min)	30 min
2	Toning Walk II (25 min) OR 15-minute Recovery Walk plus Upper Body Strength Workout	25 min	Moderate Walk (25 min) // Total-Body Strength Workout (20 min)	45 min
3	Basic Interval Walk II (45 min) // Core Strength Workout (15 min)	60 min	Supercharged Interval Walk II (30 min)	30 min
4	Toning Walk II (25 min) OR 15-minute Recovery Walk plus Upper Body Strength Workout	25 min	Recovery Walk (25 min) // Total-Body Strength Workout, 20 min	45 min
5	Basic Interval Walk II (45 min) // Lower-Body Strength Workout (15 min)	60 min	Supercharged Interval II Walk (30 min)	30 min
6	Long Walk (1–2 hours) // Core Strength Workout (15 min)	75–135 min	Speed Walk (30 min) // Total-Body Strength Workout (20 min)	<50 min
7	Rest		Rest	

>> **Do the Basic Maintenance Plan for 4 to 6 weeks.**
>> **Then do the Supercharged Maintenance Plan for the next 4 to 6 weeks.**
>> **Or alternate the plans weekly for 10 to 12 weeks.**

Continue with one or both of these cycles, trying some of the alternate toning and interval workouts for variety. See a list of alternate exercises in chapter 9 of *Walk Off Weight*.

BASIC MAINTENANCE PLAN

Each week do:

>> **90 minutes of Basic Interval Walks**
   (two 45-minute workouts or three 30-minute workouts)
>> **4 Toning Workouts (one body part will get worked twice each week,**
   so alternate which body part that is each successive week)
>> **1 Long Walk**

SUPERCHARGED MAINTENANCE PLAN

Each week do:

>> **60 minutes of Supercharged Interval Workouts**
   (two 30-minute workouts or three 20-minute workouts)
>> **30 minutes of Moderate Walking**
>> **2 Toning Workouts**
>> **1 Speed Walk**

WEEK 9
YOUR WORKOUT AT-A-GLANCE

DAY	WORKOUTS	DURATION
1		min total
2		min total
3		min total
4		min total
5		min total
6		min total
7	Rest	

WHAT YOU'LL DO THIS WEEK

- _____
- _____
- _____
- _____
- _____

THE WOW FACTOR: Post Inspiration

To keep yourself on track, place quotes in strategic spots where you might need some motivation: on the fridge, TV, dashboard, or computer. Some suggestions: "You've come too far to take orders from a cookie." "The difference between try and triumph is just a little umph!" "Do or do not. There is no try." You can find a wealth of great quotes online at sites like thinkexist.com or by searching "motivational fitness quotes" in your favorite search engine.

WORKOUT LOG

WORKOUTS	TIME	DURATION
	DAILY TOTAL EXERCISE TIME	

WORKOUT NOTES

How did you feel before? _____

_____

How did you feel after? _____

_____

Any obstacles? _____

_____

Major accomplishment? _____

_____

Other notes: _____

_____

PERSONAL NOTES

ENERGY LEVEL (circle one)
1 being "I'm so tired I can't get out of bed" and **10 being** "I could dance all night!"

1	2	3	4	5	6	7	8	9	10

SELF-ESTEEM/SELF-CONFIDENCE (circle one)
1 being "I can't do anything right" and **10 being** "I'm ready to change the world!"

1	2	3	4	5	6	7	8	9	10

FOOD LOG

	FOOD/DRINKS	TIME	CALORIES
Breakfast			
Lunch			
Snack			
Dinner			
Optional Snack			
	DAILY CALORIE TOTAL		

DAILY NUTRITION GOALS:	Grains/Starches	Fruits	Vegetables	Dairy	Healthy Fats	Lean Proteins
	☐☐☐☐☐☐	☐☐☐	☐☐☐☐☐	☐☐☐	☐☐☐☐	☐☐☐
	Water ☐☐☐☐☐	**Green Tea** ☐☐☐	*Optional* (amount per day) Fiber _____ g	**Calcium** _____ mg	**Vitamin D** _____ IU	

BONUS TRACKER *(Record your blood sugar, track your medications, gauge your hunger, or make other notes here.)*

_____

_____

_____

_____

WORKOUT LOG

WORKOUTS	TIME	DURATION
	DAILY TOTAL EXERCISE TIME	

WORKOUT NOTES

How did you feel before? _____

_____

How did you feel after? _____

_____

Any obstacles? _____

_____

Major accomplishment? _____

_____

Other notes: _____

_____

PERSONAL NOTES

ENERGY LEVEL (circle one)
1 being "I'm so tired I can't get out of bed" and **10 being** "I could dance all night!"

1	2	3	4	5	6	7	8	9	10

SELF-ESTEEM/SELF-CONFIDENCE (circle one)
1 being "I can't do anything right" and **10 being** "I'm ready to change the world!"

1	2	3	4	5	6	7	8	9	10

FOOD LOG

	FOOD/DRINKS	TIME	CALORIES
Breakfast			
Lunch			
Snack			
Dinner			
Optional Snack			
		DAILY CALORIE TOTAL	

DAILY NUTRITION GOALS:	Grains/Starches	Fruits	Vegetables	Dairy	Healthy Fats	Lean Proteins
	☐☐☐☐☐☐	☐☐☐	☐☐☐☐☐	☐☐☐	☐☐☐☐	☐☐☐
	Water	Green Tea	Optional (amount per day)			
	☐☐☐☐☐	☐☐☐	Fiber _____ g Calcium _____ mg Vitamin D _____ IU			

BONUS TRACKER (*Record your blood sugar, track your medications, gauge your hunger, or make other notes here.*)

_____

_____

_____

_____

WORKOUT LOG

WORKOUTS	TIME	DURATION
	DAILY TOTAL EXERCISE TIME	

WORKOUT NOTES

How did you feel before? _____

_____

How did you feel after? _____

_____

Any obstacles? _____

_____

Major accomplishment? _____

_____

Other notes: _____

_____

PERSONAL NOTES

ENERGY LEVEL (circle one)
1 being "I'm so tired I can't get out of bed" and **10 being** "I could dance all night!"

1	2	3	4	5	6	7	8	9	10

SELF-ESTEEM/SELF-CONFIDENCE (circle one)
1 being "I can't do anything right" and **10 being** "I'm ready to change the world!"

1	2	3	4	5	6	7	8	9	10

BEYOND 8 WEEKS WALK OFF WEIGHT

FOOD LOG

	FOOD/DRINKS	TIME	CALORIES
Breakfast			
Lunch			
Snack			
Dinner			
Optional Snack			
		DAILY CALORIE TOTAL	

DAILY NUTRITION GOALS:	Grains/Starches ☐☐☐☐☐☐	Fruits ☐☐☐	Vegetables ☐☐☐☐☐	Dairy ☐☐☐	Healthy Fats ☐☐☐☐	Lean Proteins ☐☐☐
	Water ☐☐☐☐☐	Green Tea ☐☐☐	Optional (amount per day) Fiber _____ g Calcium _____ mg Vitamin D _____ IU			

BONUS TRACKER (*Record your blood sugar, track your medications, gauge your hunger, or make other notes here.*)

_____

_____

_____

_____

WORKOUT LOG

WORKOUTS	TIME	DURATION
	DAILY TOTAL EXERCISE TIME	

WORKOUT NOTES

How did you feel before? _____

_____

How did you feel after? _____

_____

Any obstacles? _____

_____

Major accomplishment? _____

_____

Other notes: _____

_____

PERSONAL NOTES

ENERGY LEVEL (circle one)
1 being "I'm so tired I can't get out of bed" and **10 being** "I could dance all night!"

| 1 | 2 | 3 | 4 | 5 | 6 | 7 | 8 | 9 | 10 |

SELF-ESTEEM/SELF-CONFIDENCE (circle one)
1 being "I can't do anything right" and **10 being** "I'm ready to change the world!"

| 1 | 2 | 3 | 4 | 5 | 6 | 7 | 8 | 9 | 10 |

FOOD LOG

	FOOD/DRINKS	TIME	CALORIES
Breakfast			
Lunch			
Snack			
Dinner			
Optional Snack			
		DAILY CALORIE TOTAL	

DAILY NUTRITION GOALS:	Grains/Starches	Fruits	Vegetables	Dairy	Healthy Fats	Lean Proteins
	☐☐☐☐☐☐	☐☐☐	☐☐☐☐☐	☐☐☐	☐☐☐☐	☐☐☐
	Water	Green Tea	Optional (amount per day)			
	☐☐☐☐☐	☐☐☐	Fiber _____ g Calcium _____ mg Vitamin D _____ IU			

BONUS TRACKER *(Record your blood sugar, track your medications, gauge your hunger, or make other notes here.)*

_____

_____

_____

_____

169

WORKOUT LOG

WORKOUTS	TIME	DURATION
	DAILY TOTAL EXERCISE TIME	

WORKOUT NOTES

How did you feel before? _____

_____

How did you feel after? _____

_____

Any obstacles? _____

_____

Major accomplishment? _____

_____

Other notes: _____

_____

PERSONAL NOTES

ENERGY LEVEL (circle one)
1 being "I'm so tired I can't get out of bed" and **10 being** "I could dance all night!"

1	2	3	4	5	6	7	8	9	10

SELF-ESTEEM/SELF-CONFIDENCE (circle one)
1 being "I can't do anything right" and **10 being** "I'm ready to change the world!"

1	2	3	4	5	6	7	8	9	10

FOOD LOG

	FOOD/DRINKS	TIME	CALORIES
Breakfast			
Lunch			
Snack			
Dinner			
Optional Snack			
	DAILY CALORIE TOTAL		

DAILY NUTRITION GOALS:	Grains/Starches ☐☐☐☐☐☐	Fruits ☐☐☐	Vegetables ☐☐☐☐☐	Dairy ☐☐☐	Healthy Fats ☐☐☐☐	Lean Proteins ☐☐☐
	Water ☐☐☐☐☐	Green Tea ☐☐☐	*Optional* (amount per day) Fiber _____ g Calcium _____ mg **Vitamin D** _____ IU			

BONUS TRACKER *(Record your blood sugar, track your medications, gauge your hunger, or make other notes here.)*

_____

_____

_____

_____

171

WORKOUT LOG

WORKOUTS	TIME	DURATION
	DAILY TOTAL EXERCISE TIME	

WORKOUT NOTES

How did you feel before? _____

_____

How did you feel after? _____

_____

Any obstacles? _____

_____

Major accomplishment? _____

_____

Other notes: _____

_____

PERSONAL NOTES

ENERGY LEVEL (circle one)
1 being "I'm so tired I can't get out of bed" and **10 being** "I could dance all night!"

1	2	3	4	5	6	7	8	9	10

SELF-ESTEEM/SELF-CONFIDENCE (circle one)
1 being "I can't do anything right" and **10 being** "I'm ready to change the world!"

1	2	3	4	5	6	7	8	9	10

FOOD LOG

	FOOD/DRINKS	TIME	CALORIES
Breakfast			
Lunch			
Snack			
Dinner			
Optional Snack			
		DAILY CALORIE TOTAL	

DAILY NUTRITION GOALS:	Grains/Starches	Fruits	Vegetables	Dairy	Healthy Fats	Lean Proteins
	☐☐☐☐☐☐	☐☐☐	☐☐☐☐☐	☐☐☐	☐☐☐☐	☐☐☐
	Water	Green Tea	Optional (amount per day)			
	☐☐☐☐☐	☐☐☐	Fiber _____ g Calcium _____ mg **Vitamin D** _____ IU			

BONUS TRACKER (*Record your blood sugar, track your medications, gauge your hunger, or make other notes here.*)

_____

_____

_____

_____

WORKOUT LOG

WORKOUTS	TIME	DURATION
	DAILY TOTAL EXERCISE TIME	

WORKOUT NOTES

How did you feel before? _____

_____

How did you feel after? _____

_____

Any obstacles? _____

_____

Major accomplishment? _____

_____

Other notes: _____

_____

PERSONAL NOTES

ENERGY LEVEL (circle one)
1 being "I'm so tired I can't get out of bed" and **10 being** "I could dance all night!"

1	2	3	4	5	6	7	8	9	10

SELF-ESTEEM/SELF-CONFIDENCE (circle one)
1 being "I can't do anything right" and **10 being** "I'm ready to change the world!"

1	2	3	4	5	6	7	8	9	10

FOOD LOG

	FOOD/DRINKS	TIME	CALORIES
Breakfast			
Lunch			
Snack			
Dinner			
Optional Snack			
		DAILY CALORIE TOTAL	

DAILY NUTRITION GOALS:	Grains/Starches ☐☐☐☐☐☐	Fruits ☐☐☐	Vegetables ☐☐☐☐☐	Dairy ☐☐☐	Healthy Fats ☐☐☐☐	Lean Proteins ☐☐☐
	Water ☐☐☐☐☐	Green Tea ☐☐☐	Optional (amount per day) Fiber _____ g Calcium _____ mg **Vitamin D** _____ IU			

BONUS TRACKER *(Record your blood sugar, track your medications, gauge your hunger, or make other notes here.)*

_____

_____

_____

_____

WEEKLY MEASUREMENTS LOG

WEIGHT _____
LBS

INCHES

_____   _____   _____

CHEST   LEFT THIGH   RIGHT THIGH

_____   _____   _____

WAIST   LEFT BICEPS   RIGHT BICEPS

_____

HIPS (at fullest part)

PERSONAL NOTES

ENERGY LEVEL (circle one)
1 being "I'm so tired I can't get out of bed" and **10 being** "I could dance all night!"

| 1 | 2 | 3 | 4 | 5 | 6 | 7 | 8 | 9 | 10 |

SELF-ESTEEM/SELF-CONFIDENCE (circle one)
1 being "I can't do anything right" and **10 being** "I'm ready to change the world!"

| 1 | 2 | 3 | 4 | 5 | 6 | 7 | 8 | 9 | 10 |

WEEK 10
YOUR WORKOUT AT-A-GLANCE

DAY	WORKOUTS	DURATION
1		min total
2		min total
3		min total
4		min total
5		min total
6		min total
7	Rest	

||||||||||||||||||||||||||||||||||||||||||||||||||||||||||||||||||||||||||||||||||||||||||||||||||||||

WHAT YOU'LL **DO THIS WEEK**

- _____
- _____
- _____
- _____
- _____

||||||||||||||||||||||||||||||||||||||||||||||||||||||||||||||||||||||||||||||||||||||||||||||||||||||

THE WOW FACTOR: Sit Down and Savor Your Meal

When you're stressed, you tend to gulp down your food, eating more than if you were savoring every bite. A study at Brazosport Memorial Hospital in Lake Jackson, TX, found that when six women were asked to eat slowly, chew thoroughly, and stop when their food no longer tasted as good as when they took their first bite, they lost, on average, 8 pounds in about a month, which they maintained over the year long study. A control group averaged a 3 pound weight gain.

Poothullil, JM. "Recognition of oral sensory satisfaction and regulation of the volume of intake in humans." *Nutritional Neuroscience* (2005), 8(4): 245-250

WORKOUT LOG

WORKOUTS	TIME	DURATION
	DAILY TOTAL EXERCISE TIME	

WORKOUT NOTES

How did you feel before? _____

_____

How did you feel after? _____

_____

Any obstacles? _____

_____

Major accomplishment? _____

_____

Other notes: _____

_____

PERSONAL NOTES

ENERGY LEVEL (circle one)
1 being "I'm so tired I can't get out of bed" and **10 being** "I could dance all night!"

1	2	3	4	5	6	7	8	9	10

SELF-ESTEEM/SELF-CONFIDENCE (circle one)
1 being "I can't do anything right" and **10 being** "I'm ready to change the world!"

1	2	3	4	5	6	7	8	9	10

FOOD LOG

	FOOD/DRINKS	TIME	CALORIES
Breakfast			
Lunch			
Snack			
Dinner			
Optional Snack			
		DAILY CALORIE TOTAL	

DAILY NUTRITION GOALS:	Grains/Starches ☐☐☐☐☐☐	Fruits ☐☐☐	Vegetables ☐☐☐☐☐	Dairy ☐☐☐	Healthy Fats ☐☐☐☐	Lean Proteins ☐☐☐
	Water ☐☐☐☐☐	Green Tea ☐☐☐	Optional (amount per day) Fiber ____g Calcium ____mg Vitamin D ____IU			

BONUS TRACKER *(Record your blood sugar, track your medications, gauge your hunger, or make other notes here.)*

_____

_____

_____

_____

179

WORKOUT LOG

WORKOUTS	TIME	DURATION
	DAILY TOTAL EXERCISE TIME	

WORKOUT NOTES

How did you feel before? _____

_____

How did you feel after? _____

_____

Any obstacles? _____

_____

Major accomplishment? _____

_____

Other notes: _____

_____

PERSONAL NOTES

ENERGY LEVEL (circle one)
1 being "I'm so tired I can't get out of bed" and **10 being** "I could dance all night!"

1	2	3	4	5	6	7	8	9	10

SELF-ESTEEM/SELF-CONFIDENCE (circle one)
1 being "I can't do anything right" and **10 being** "I'm ready to change the world!"

1	2	3	4	5	6	7	8	9	10

FOOD LOG

	FOOD/DRINKS	TIME	CALORIES
Breakfast			
Lunch			
Snack			
Dinner			
Optional Snack			
	DAILY CALORIE TOTAL		

DAILY NUTRITION GOALS:	Grains/Starches	Fruits	Vegetables	Dairy	Healthy Fats	Lean Proteins
	☐☐☐☐☐☐	☐☐☐	☐☐☐☐☐	☐☐☐	☐☐☐☐	☐☐☐
	Water	Green Tea	Optional (amount per day)			
	☐☐☐☐☐	☐☐☐	Fiber _____ g Calcium _____ mg **Vitamin D** _____ IU			

BONUS TRACKER (*Record your blood sugar, track your medications, gauge your hunger, or make other notes here.*)

_____

_____

_____

_____

WORKOUT LOG

WORKOUTS	TIME	DURATION
	DAILY TOTAL EXERCISE TIME	

WORKOUT NOTES

How did you feel before? _____

_____

How did you feel after? _____

_____

Any obstacles? _____

_____

Major accomplishment? _____

_____

Other notes: _____

_____

PERSONAL NOTES

ENERGY LEVEL (circle one)
1 being "I'm so tired I can't get out of bed" and **10 being** "I could dance all night!"

1	2	3	4	5	6	7	8	9	10

SELF-ESTEEM/SELF-CONFIDENCE (circle one)
1 being "I can't do anything right" and **10 being** "I'm ready to change the world!"

1	2	3	4	5	6	7	8	9	10

FOOD LOG

	FOOD/DRINKS	TIME	CALORIES
Breakfast			
Lunch			
Snack			
Dinner			
Optional Snack			
	DAILY CALORIE TOTAL		

DAILY NUTRITION GOALS:	Grains/Starches ☐☐☐☐☐☐	Fruits ☐☐☐	Vegetables ☐☐☐☐☐	Dairy ☐☐☐	Healthy Fats ☐☐☐☐	Lean Proteins ☐☐☐
	Water ☐☐☐☐☐	Green Tea ☐☐☐	Optional (amount per day) Fiber ____g Calcium ____mg Vitamin D ____IU			

BONUS TRACKER (Record your blood sugar, track your medications, gauge your hunger, or make other notes here.)

_____

_____

_____

_____

183

WORKOUT LOG

WORKOUTS	TIME	DURATION
	DAILY TOTAL EXERCISE TIME	

WORKOUT NOTES

How did you feel before? _____

_____

How did you feel after? _____

_____

Any obstacles? _____

_____

Major accomplishment? _____

_____

Other notes: _____

_____

PERSONAL NOTES

ENERGY LEVEL (circle one)
1 being "I'm so tired I can't get out of bed" and **10 being** "I could dance all night!"

1	2	3	4	5	6	7	8	9	10

SELF-ESTEEM/SELF-CONFIDENCE (circle one)
1 being "I can't do anything right" and **10 being** "I'm ready to change the world!"

1	2	3	4	5	6	7	8	9	10

FOOD LOG

	FOOD/DRINKS	TIME	CALORIES
Breakfast			
Lunch			
Snack			
Dinner			
Optional Snack			
	DAILY CALORIE TOTAL		

DAILY NUTRITION GOALS:	Grains/Starches ☐☐☐☐☐☐	Fruits ☐☐☐	Vegetables ☐☐☐☐☐	Dairy ☐☐☐	Healthy Fats ☐☐☐☐	Lean Proteins ☐☐☐
	Water ☐☐☐☐☐	Green Tea ☐☐☐	Optional (amount per day) Fiber _____ g Calcium _____ mg Vitamin D _____ IU			

BONUS TRACKER (*Record your blood sugar, track your medications, gauge your hunger, or make other notes here.*)

_____

_____

_____

_____

WORKOUT LOG

WORKOUTS	TIME	DURATION
	DAILY TOTAL EXERCISE TIME	

WORKOUT NOTES

How did you feel before? _____

_____

How did you feel after? _____

_____

Any obstacles? _____

_____

Major accomplishment? _____

_____

Other notes: _____

_____

PERSONAL NOTES

ENERGY LEVEL (circle one)
1 being "I'm so tired I can't get out of bed" and **10 being** "I could dance all night!"

1	2	3	4	5	6	7	8	9	10

SELF-ESTEEM/SELF-CONFIDENCE (circle one)
1 being "I can't do anything right" and **10 being** "I'm ready to change the world!"

1	2	3	4	5	6	7	8	9	10

FOOD LOG

	FOOD/DRINKS	TIME	CALORIES
Breakfast			
Lunch			
Snack			
Dinner			
Optional Snack			
	DAILY CALORIE TOTAL		

DAILY NUTRITION GOALS:	Grains/Starches	Fruits	Vegetables	Dairy	Healthy Fats	Lean Proteins
	☐☐☐☐☐☐	☐☐☐	☐☐☐☐☐	☐☐☐	☐☐☐☐	☐☐☐
	Water	**Green Tea**	*Optional* (amount per day)			
	☐☐☐☐☐	☐☐☐	Fiber _____ g Calcium _____ mg Vitamin D _____ IU			

BONUS TRACKER *(Record your blood sugar, track your medications, gauge your hunger, or make other notes here.)*

_____

_____

_____

_____

WORKOUT LOG

WORKOUTS	TIME	DURATION
	DAILY TOTAL EXERCISE TIME	

WORKOUT NOTES

How did you feel before? _____

_____

How did you feel after? _____

_____

Any obstacles? _____

_____

Major accomplishment? _____

_____

Other notes: _____

_____

PERSONAL NOTES

ENERGY LEVEL (circle one)
1 being "I'm so tired I can't get out of bed" and **10 being** "I could dance all night!"

1	2	3	4	5	6	7	8	9	10

SELF-ESTEEM/SELF-CONFIDENCE (circle one)
1 being "I can't do anything right" and **10 being** "I'm ready to change the world!"

1	2	3	4	5	6	7	8	9	10

FOOD LOG

	FOOD/DRINKS	TIME	CALORIES
Breakfast			
Lunch			
Snack			
Dinner			
Optional Snack			
		DAILY CALORIE TOTAL	

DAILY NUTRITION GOALS:	Grains/Starches	Fruits	Vegetables	Dairy	Healthy Fats	Lean Proteins
	☐☐☐☐☐☐	☐☐☐	☐☐☐☐☐	☐☐☐	☐☐☐☐	☐☐☐
	Water	**Green Tea**	*Optional* (amount per day)			
	☐☐☐☐☐	☐☐☐	**Fiber** _____ g **Calcium** _____ mg **Vitamin D** _____ IU			

BONUS TRACKER *(Record your blood sugar, track your medications, gauge your hunger, or make other notes here.)*

_____

_____

_____

_____

WORKOUT LOG

WORKOUTS	TIME	DURATION
	DAILY TOTAL EXERCISE TIME	

WORKOUT NOTES

How did you feel before? _____

_____

How did you feel after? _____

_____

Any obstacles? _____

_____

Major accomplishment? _____

_____

Other notes: _____

_____

PERSONAL NOTES

ENERGY LEVEL (circle one)
1 being "I'm so tired I can't get out of bed" and **10 being** "I could dance all night!"

1	2	3	4	5	6	7	8	9	10

SELF-ESTEEM/SELF-CONFIDENCE (circle one)
1 being "I can't do anything right" and **10 being** "I'm ready to change the world!"

1	2	3	4	5	6	7	8	9	10

FOOD LOG

	FOOD/DRINKS	TIME	CALORIES
Breakfast			
Lunch			
Snack			
Dinner			
Optional Snack			
		DAILY CALORIE TOTAL	

DAILY NUTRITION GOALS:	Grains/Starches	Fruits	Vegetables	Dairy	Healthy Fats	Lean Proteins
	☐☐☐☐☐☐	☐☐☐	☐☐☐☐☐	☐☐☐	☐☐☐☐	☐☐☐
	Water	Green Tea	Optional (amount per day)			
	☐☐☐☐☐	☐☐☐	Fiber _____ g Calcium _____ mg Vitamin D _____ IU			

BONUS TRACKER *(Record your blood sugar, track your medications, gauge your hunger, or make other notes here.)*

_____

_____

_____

_____

WEEKLY MEASUREMENTS LOG

WEIGHT _____
LBS

INCHES _____   _____   _____
CHEST   LEFT THIGH   RIGHT THIGH

_____   _____   _____
WAIST   LEFT BICEPS   RIGHT BICEPS

_____
HIPS (at fullest part)

PERSONAL NOTES
ENERGY LEVEL (circle one)
1 being "I'm so tired I can't get out of bed" and **10 being** "I could dance all night!"

1	2	3	4	5	6	7	8	9	10

SELF-ESTEEM/SELF-CONFIDENCE (circle one)
1 being "I can't do anything right" and **10 being** "I'm ready to change the world!"

1	2	3	4	5	6	7	8	9	10

WEEK 11
YOUR WORKOUT AT-A-GLANCE

DAY	WORKOUTS	DURATION
1		min total
2		min total
3		min total
4		min total
5		min total
6		min total
7	Rest	

WHAT YOU'LL **DO THIS WEEK**

- _____
- _____
- _____
- _____
- _____

THE WOW FACTOR: Stand Up Straight

Don't trudge through your workouts with slumped shoulders. Whether you're walking or lifting weights, research shows that working out with proper posture can burn more calories and safeguard you from injury. It also allows you to take in more oxygen—making a workout feel easier. *Bonus:* You'll look slimmer.

WORKOUT LOG

WORKOUTS	TIME	DURATION
	DAILY TOTAL EXERCISE TIME	

WORKOUT NOTES

How did you feel before? _____

_____

How did you feel after? _____

_____

Any obstacles? _____

_____

Major accomplishment? _____

_____

Other notes: _____

_____

PERSONAL NOTES

ENERGY LEVEL (circle one)
1 being "I'm so tired I can't get out of bed" and **10 being** "I could dance all night!"

1	2	3	4	5	6	7	8	9	10

SELF-ESTEEM/SELF-CONFIDENCE (circle one)
1 being "I can't do anything right" and **10 being** "I'm ready to change the world!"

1	2	3	4	5	6	7	8	9	10

FOOD LOG

	FOOD/DRINKS	TIME	CALORIES
Breakfast			
Lunch			
Snack			
Dinner			
Optional Snack			
		DAILY CALORIE TOTAL	

DAILY NUTRITION GOALS:	Grains/Starches ☐☐☐☐☐☐	Fruits ☐☐☐	Vegetables ☐☐☐☐☐	Dairy ☐☐☐	Healthy Fats ☐☐☐☐	Lean Proteins ☐☐☐
	Water ☐☐☐☐☐	Green Tea ☐☐☐	Optional (amount per day) Fiber ____ g Calcium ____ mg Vitamin D ____ IU			

BONUS TRACKER (*Record your blood sugar, track your medications, gauge your hunger, or make other notes here.*)

_____

_____

_____

_____

WORKOUT LOG

WORKOUTS	TIME	DURATION
	DAILY TOTAL EXERCISE TIME	

WORKOUT NOTES

How did you feel before? _____

_____

How did you feel after? _____

_____

Any obstacles? _____

_____

Major accomplishment? _____

_____

Other notes: _____

_____

PERSONAL NOTES

ENERGY LEVEL (circle one)
1 being "I'm so tired I can't get out of bed" and **10 being** "I could dance all night!"

1	2	3	4	5	6	7	8	9	10

SELF-ESTEEM/SELF-CONFIDENCE (circle one)
1 being "I can't do anything right" and **10 being** "I'm ready to change the world!"

1	2	3	4	5	6	7	8	9	10

FOOD LOG

	FOOD/DRINKS	TIME	CALORIES
Breakfast			
Lunch			
Snack			
Dinner			
Optional Snack			
		DAILY CALORIE TOTAL	

| **DAILY NUTRITION GOALS:** | Grains/Starches   Fruits   Vegetables   Dairy   Healthy Fats   Lean Proteins
 ☐☐☐☐☐☐   ☐☐☐   ☐☐☐☐☐   ☐☐☐   ☐☐☐☐   ☐☐☐
 Water   Green Tea   *Optional* (amount per day)
 ☐☐☐☐☐   ☐☐☐   **Fiber** _____ g   **Calcium** _____ mg   **Vitamin D** _____ IU |

BONUS TRACKER *(Record your blood sugar, track your medications, gauge your hunger, or make other notes here.)*

_____

_____

_____

_____

WORKOUT LOG

WORKOUTS	TIME	DURATION
	DAILY TOTAL EXERCISE TIME	

WORKOUT NOTES

How did you feel before? _____

_____

How did you feel after? _____

_____

Any obstacles? _____

_____

Major accomplishment? _____

_____

Other notes: _____

_____

PERSONAL NOTES

ENERGY LEVEL (circle one)
1 being "I'm so tired I can't get out of bed" and **10 being** "I could dance all night!"

1	2	3	4	5	6	7	8	9	10

SELF-ESTEEM/SELF-CONFIDENCE (circle one)
1 being "I can't do anything right" and **10 being** "I'm ready to change the world!"

1	2	3	4	5	6	7	8	9	10

FOOD LOG

	FOOD/DRINKS	TIME	CALORIES
Breakfast			
Lunch			
Snack			
Dinner			
Optional Snack			
	DAILY CALORIE TOTAL		

DAILY NUTRITION GOALS:	Grains/Starches ☐☐☐☐☐☐	Fruits ☐☐☐	Vegetables ☐☐☐☐☐	Dairy ☐☐☐	Healthy Fats ☐☐☐☐	Lean Proteins ☐☐☐
	Water ☐☐☐☐☐	Green Tea ☐☐☐	Optional (amount per day) Fiber _____ g Calcium _____ mg Vitamin D _____ IU			

BONUS TRACKER *(Record your blood sugar, track your medications, gauge your hunger, or make other notes here.)*

_____

_____

_____

_____

199

WORKOUT LOG

WORKOUTS	TIME	DURATION
	DAILY TOTAL EXERCISE TIME	

WORKOUT NOTES

How did you feel before? _____

_____

How did you feel after? _____

_____

Any obstacles? _____

_____

Major accomplishment? _____

_____

Other notes: _____

_____

PERSONAL NOTES

ENERGY LEVEL (circle one)
1 being "I'm so tired I can't get out of bed" and **10 being** "I could dance all night!"

1	2	3	4	5	6	7	8	9	10

SELF-ESTEEM/SELF-CONFIDENCE (circle one)
1 being "I can't do anything right" and **10 being** "I'm ready to change the world!"

1	2	3	4	5	6	7	8	9	10

FOOD LOG

	FOOD/DRINKS	TIME	CALORIES
Breakfast			
Lunch			
Snack			
Dinner			
Optional Snack			
		DAILY CALORIE TOTAL	

DAILY NUTRITION GOALS:	Grains/Starches	Fruits	Vegetables	Dairy	Healthy Fats	Lean Proteins
	☐☐☐☐☐☐	☐☐☐	☐☐☐☐☐	☐☐☐	☐☐☐☐	☐☐☐
	Water	Green Tea	Optional (amount per day)			
	☐☐☐☐☐	☐☐☐	Fiber _____ g Calcium _____ mg Vitamin D _____ IU			

BONUS TRACKER (*Record your blood sugar, track your medications, gauge your hunger, or make other notes here.*)

_____

_____

_____

_____

WORKOUT LOG

WORKOUTS	TIME	DURATION
	DAILY TOTAL EXERCISE TIME	

WORKOUT NOTES

How did you feel before? _____

_____

How did you feel after? _____

_____

Any obstacles? _____

_____

Major accomplishment? _____

_____

Other notes: _____

_____

PERSONAL NOTES

ENERGY LEVEL (circle one)
1 being "I'm so tired I can't get out of bed" and **10 being** "I could dance all night!"

1	2	3	4	5	6	7	8	9	10

SELF-ESTEEM/SELF-CONFIDENCE (circle one)
1 being "I can't do anything right" and **10 being** "I'm ready to change the world!"

1	2	3	4	5	6	7	8	9	10

FOOD LOG

	FOOD/DRINKS	TIME	CALORIES
Breakfast			
Lunch			
Snack			
Dinner			
Optional Snack			
	DAILY CALORIE TOTAL		

DAILY NUTRITION GOALS:

Grains/Starches	Fruits	Vegetables	Dairy	Healthy Fats	Lean Proteins
☐☐☐☐☐☐	☐☐☐	☐☐☐☐☐	☐☐☐	☐☐☐☐	☐☐☐

Water	Green Tea	Optional (amount per day)
☐☐☐☐☐	☐☐☐	Fiber _____ g Calcium _____ mg **Vitamin D** _____ IU

BONUS TRACKER (*Record your blood sugar, track your medications, gauge your hunger, or make other notes here.*)

_____

_____

_____

_____

WORKOUT LOG

WORKOUTS	TIME	DURATION
	DAILY TOTAL EXERCISE TIME	

WORKOUT NOTES

How did you feel before? _____

_____

How did you feel after? _____

_____

Any obstacles? _____

_____

Major accomplishment? _____

_____

Other notes: _____

_____

PERSONAL NOTES

ENERGY LEVEL (circle one)
1 being "I'm so tired I can't get out of bed" and **10 being** "I could dance all night!"

1	2	3	4	5	6	7	8	9	10

SELF-ESTEEM/SELF-CONFIDENCE (circle one)
1 being "I can't do anything right" and **10 being** "I'm ready to change the world!"

1	2	3	4	5	6	7	8	9	10

FOOD LOG

	FOOD/DRINKS	TIME	CALORIES
Breakfast			
Lunch			
Snack			
Dinner			
Optional Snack			
		DAILY CALORIE TOTAL	

DAILY NUTRITION GOALS:	Grains/Starches	Fruits	Vegetables	Dairy	Healthy Fats	Lean Proteins
	☐☐☐☐☐☐	☐☐☐	☐☐☐☐☐	☐☐☐	☐☐☐☐	☐☐☐
	Water	Green Tea	*Optional* (amount per day)			
	☐☐☐☐☐	☐☐☐	Fiber _____g Calcium _____mg Vitamin D _____IU			

BONUS TRACKER *(Record your blood sugar, track your medications, gauge your hunger, or make other notes here.)*

_____

_____

_____

_____

WORKOUT LOG

WORKOUTS	TIME	DURATION
	DAILY TOTAL EXERCISE TIME	

WORKOUT NOTES

How did you feel before? _____

_____

How did you feel after? _____

_____

Any obstacles? _____

_____

Major accomplishment? _____

_____

Other notes: _____

_____

PERSONAL NOTES

ENERGY LEVEL (circle one)
1 being "I'm so tired I can't get out of bed" and **10 being** "I could dance all night!"

1	2	3	4	5	6	7	8	9	10

SELF-ESTEEM/SELF-CONFIDENCE (circle one)
1 being "I can't do anything right" and **10 being** "I'm ready to change the world!"

1	2	3	4	5	6	7	8	9	10

FOOD LOG

	FOOD/DRINKS	TIME	CALORIES
Breakfast			
Lunch			
Snack			
Dinner			
Optional Snack			
	DAILY CALORIE TOTAL		

DAILY NUTRITION GOALS:	Grains/Starches ☐☐☐☐☐☐	Fruits ☐☐☐	Vegetables ☐☐☐☐☐	Dairy ☐☐☐	Healthy Fats ☐☐☐☐	Lean Proteins ☐☐☐
	Water ☐☐☐☐☐	Green Tea ☐☐☐	Optional (amount per day) Fiber _____ g Calcium _____ mg Vitamin D _____ IU			

BONUS TRACKER (*Record your blood sugar, track your medications, gauge your hunger, or make other notes here.*)

_____

_____

_____

_____

DATE/TIME _____

WEEKLY MEASUREMENTS LOG

WEIGHT _____
LBS

INCHES _____ _____ _____
CHEST   LEFT THIGH   RIGHT THIGH

_____ _____ _____
WAIST   LEFT BICEPS   RIGHT BICEPS

_____
HIPS (at fullest part)

PERSONAL NOTES

ENERGY LEVEL (circle one)
1 being "I'm so tired I can't get out of bed" and **10 being** "I could dance all night!"

| 1 | 2 | 3 | 4 | 5 | 6 | 7 | 8 | 9 | 10 |

SELF-ESTEEM/SELF-CONFIDENCE (circle one)
1 being "I can't do anything right" and **10 being** "I'm ready to change the world!"

| 1 | 2 | 3 | 4 | 5 | 6 | 7 | 8 | 9 | 10 |

WEEK 12
YOUR WORKOUT AT-A-GLANCE

DAY	WORKOUTS	DURATION
1		min total
2		min total
3		min total
4		min total
5		min total
6		min total
7	Rest	

WHAT YOU'LL **DO THIS WEEK**

- _____
- _____
- _____
- _____
- _____

THE WOW FACTOR: Exercise to Spice Up Your Love Life

Forget the pillow talk: Research from the University of Washington found that a single 20-minute cycling workout boosted sexual arousal in women by up to 169%. Exercise increases blood flow to the genitals. A walk can provide a pre-romp warm-up, too.

Meston CM, Gorzalka BB. "Differential effects of sympathetic activation on sexual arousal in sexually dysfunctional and functional women." *Journal of Abnormal Psychology* (1996), 105: 582–591

WORKOUT LOG

WORKOUTS	TIME	DURATION
	DAILY TOTAL EXERCISE TIME	

WORKOUT NOTES

How did you feel before? _____

_____

How did you feel after? _____

_____

Any obstacles? _____

_____

Major accomplishment? _____

_____

Other notes: _____

_____

PERSONAL NOTES

ENERGY LEVEL (circle one)
1 being "I'm so tired I can't get out of bed" and **10 being** "I could dance all night!"

1	2	3	4	5	6	7	8	9	10

SELF ESTEEM/SELF-CONFIDENCE (circle one)
1 being "I can't do anything right" and **10 being** "I'm ready to change the world!"

1	2	3	4	5	6	7	8	9	10

FOOD LOG

	FOOD/DRINKS	TIME	CALORIES
Breakfast			
Lunch			
Snack			
Dinner			
Optional Snack			
		DAILY CALORIE TOTAL	

DAILY NUTRITION GOALS:	Grains/Starches	Fruits	Vegetables	Dairy	Healthy Fats	Lean Proteins
	☐☐☐☐☐☐	☐☐☐	☐☐☐☐☐	☐☐☐	☐☐☐☐	☐☐☐
	Water	Green Tea	Optional (amount per day)			
	☐☐☐☐☐	☐☐☐	Fiber _____ g Calcium _____ mg **Vitamin D** _____ IU			

BONUS TRACKER *(Record your blood sugar, track your medications, gauge your hunger, or make other notes here.)*

_____

_____

_____

_____

WORKOUT LOG

WORKOUTS	TIME	DURATION
	DAILY TOTAL EXERCISE TIME	

WORKOUT NOTES

How did you feel before? _____

_____

How did you feel after? _____

_____

Any obstacles? _____

_____

Major accomplishment? _____

_____

Other notes: _____

_____

PERSONAL NOTES

ENERGY LEVEL (circle one)
1 being "I'm so tired I can't get out of bed" and **10 being** "I could dance all night!"

1	2	3	4	5	6	7	8	9	10

SELF ESTEEM/SELF-CONFIDENCE (circle one)
1 being "I can't do anything right" and **10 being** "I'm ready to change the world!"

1	2	3	4	5	6	7	8	9	10

FOOD LOG

	FOOD/DRINKS	TIME	CALORIES
Breakfast			
Lunch			
Snack			
Dinner			
Optional Snack			
		DAILY CALORIE TOTAL	

DAILY NUTRITION GOALS:

Grains/Starches ☐☐☐☐☐☐ Fruits ☐☐☐ Vegetables ☐☐☐☐☐ Dairy ☐☐☐ Healthy Fats ☐☐☐☐ Lean Proteins ☐☐☐

Water ☐☐☐☐☐ Green Tea ☐☐☐ Optional (amount per day) Fiber _____ g Calcium _____ mg Vitamin D _____ IU

BONUS TRACKER (Record your blood sugar, track your medications, gauge your hunger, or make other notes here.)

_____
_____
_____
_____

WORKOUT LOG

WORKOUTS	TIME	DURATION
	DAILY TOTAL EXERCISE TIME	

WORKOUT NOTES

How did you feel before? _____

_____

How did you feel after? _____

_____

Any obstacles? _____

_____

Major accomplishment? _____

_____

Other notes: _____

_____

PERSONAL NOTES

ENERGY LEVEL (circle one)
1 being "I'm so tired I can't get out of bed" and **10 being** "I could dance all night!"

1	2	3	4	5	6	7	8	9	10

SELF ESTEEM/SELF-CONFIDENCE (circle one)
1 being "I can't do anything right" and **10 being** "I'm ready to change the world!"

1	2	3	4	5	6	7	8	9	10

FOOD LOG

	FOOD/DRINKS	TIME	CALORIES
Breakfast			
Lunch			
Snack			
Dinner			
Optional Snack			
		DAILY CALORIE TOTAL	

DAILY NUTRITION GOALS:	Grains/Starches □□□□□□	Fruits □□□	Vegetables □□□□□	Dairy □□□	Healthy Fats □□□□	Lean Proteins □□□
	Water □□□□□	Green Tea □□□	Optional (amount per day) Fiber _____ g Calcium _____ mg **Vitamin D** _____ IU			

BONUS TRACKER (*Record your blood sugar, track your medications, gauge your hunger, or make other notes here.*)

_____

_____

_____

_____

WORKOUT LOG

WORKOUTS	TIME	DURATION
	DAILY TOTAL EXERCISE TIME	

WORKOUT NOTES

How did you feel before? _____

_____

How did you feel after? _____

_____

Any obstacles? _____

_____

Major accomplishment? _____

_____

Other notes: _____

_____

PERSONAL NOTES

ENERGY LEVEL (circle one)
1 being "I'm so tired I can't get out of bed" and **10 being** "I could dance all night!"

1	2	3	4	5	6	7	8	9	10

SELF ESTEEM/SELF-CONFIDENCE (circle one)
1 being "I can't do anything right" and **10 being** "I'm ready to change the world!"

1	2	3	4	5	6	7	8	9	10

FOOD LOG

	FOOD/DRINKS	TIME	CALORIES
Breakfast			
Lunch			
Snack			
Dinner			
Optional Snack			
		DAILY CALORIE TOTAL	

DAILY NUTRITION GOALS:	Grains/Starches	Fruits	Vegetables	Dairy	Healthy Fats	Lean Proteins
	☐☐☐☐☐☐	☐☐☐	☐☐☐☐☐	☐☐☐	☐☐☐☐	☐☐☐
	Water	Green Tea	Optional (amount per day)			
	☐☐☐☐☐	☐☐☐	Fiber _____ g Calcium _____ mg Vitamin D _____ IU			

BONUS TRACKER (*Record your blood sugar, track your medications, gauge your hunger, or make other notes here.*)

_____

_____

_____

_____

217

WORKOUT LOG

WORKOUTS	TIME	DURATION
	DAILY TOTAL EXERCISE TIME	

WORKOUT NOTES

How did you feel before? _____

_____

How did you feel after? _____

_____

Any obstacles? _____

_____

Major accomplishment? _____

_____

Other notes: _____

_____

PERSONAL NOTES

ENERGY LEVEL (circle one)
1 being "I'm so tired I can't get out of bed" and **10 being** "I could dance all night!"

1	2	3	4	5	6	7	8	9	10

SELF ESTEEM/SELF-CONFIDENCE (circle one)
1 being "I can't do anything right" and **10 being** "I'm ready to change the world!"

1	2	3	4	5	6	7	8	9	10

FOOD LOG

	FOOD/DRINKS	TIME	CALORIES
Breakfast			
Lunch			
Snack			
Dinner			
Optional Snack			
		DAILY CALORIE TOTAL	

DAILY NUTRITION GOALS:	Grains/Starches	Fruits	Vegetables	Dairy	Healthy Fats	Lean Proteins
	☐☐☐☐☐☐	☐☐☐	☐☐☐☐☐	☐☐☐	☐☐☐☐	☐☐☐
	Water	Green Tea	Optional (amount per day)			
	☐☐☐☐☐	☐☐☐	Fiber _____ g Calcium _____ mg Vitamin D _____ IU			

BONUS TRACKER (*Record your blood sugar, track your medications, gauge your hunger, or make other notes here.*)

_____

_____

_____

_____

219

WORKOUT LOG

WORKOUTS	TIME	DURATION
	DAILY TOTAL EXERCISE TIME	

WORKOUT NOTES

How did you feel before? _____

_____

How did you feel after? _____

_____

Any obstacles? _____

_____

Major accomplishment? _____

_____

Other notes: _____

_____

PERSONAL NOTES

ENERGY LEVEL (circle one)
1 being "I'm so tired I can't get out of bed" and **10 being** "I could dance all night!"

1	2	3	4	5	6	7	8	9	10

SELF ESTEEM/SELF-CONFIDENCE (circle one)
1 being "I can't do anything right" and **10 being** "I'm ready to change the world!"

1	2	3	4	5	6	7	8	9	10

FOOD LOG

	FOOD/DRINKS	TIME	CALORIES
Breakfast			
Lunch			
Snack			
Dinner			
Optional Snack			
	DAILY CALORIE TOTAL		

DAILY NUTRITION GOALS:	Grains/Starches ☐☐☐☐☐☐	Fruits ☐☐☐	Vegetables ☐☐☐☐☐	Dairy ☐☐☐	Healthy Fats ☐☐☐☐	Lean Proteins ☐☐☐
	Water ☐☐☐☐☐	Green Tea ☐☐☐	Optional (amount per day) Fiber _____ g Calcium _____ mg Vitamin D _____ IU			

BONUS TRACKER *(Record your blood sugar, track your medications, gauge your hunger, or make other notes here.)*

_____

_____

_____

_____

221

WORKOUT LOG

WORKOUTS	TIME	DURATION
	DAILY TOTAL EXERCISE TIME	

WORKOUT NOTES

How did you feel before? _____

_____

How did you feel after? _____

_____

Any obstacles? _____

_____

Major accomplishment? _____

_____

Other notes: _____

_____

PERSONAL NOTES

ENERGY LEVEL (circle one)
1 being "I'm so tired I can't get out of bed" and **10 being** "I could dance all night!"

1	2	3	4	5	6	7	8	9	10

SELF ESTEEM/SELF-CONFIDENCE (circle one)
1 being "I can't do anything right" and **10 being** "I'm ready to change the world!"

1	2	3	4	5	6	7	8	9	10

FOOD LOG

	FOOD/DRINKS	TIME	CALORIES
Breakfast			
Lunch			
Snack			
Dinner			
Optional Snack			
	DAILY CALORIE TOTAL		

DAILY NUTRITION GOALS:	Grains/Starches	Fruits	Vegetables	Dairy	Healthy Fats	Lean Proteins
	☐☐☐☐☐☐	☐☐☐	☐☐☐☐☐	☐☐☐	☐☐☐☐	☐☐☐
	Water	Green Tea	Optional (amount per day)			
	☐☐☐☐☐	☐☐☐	Fiber _____g Calcium _____mg **Vitamin D** _____IU			

BONUS TRACKER *(Record your blood sugar, track your medications, gauge your hunger, or make other notes here.)*

_____

_____

_____

_____

WEEKLY MEASUREMENTS LOG

WEIGHT _____
LBS

INCHES _____   _____   _____
              CHEST   LEFT THIGH   RIGHT THIGH

                _____   _____   _____
              WAIST   LEFT BICEPS   RIGHT BICEPS

                _____
              HIPS (at fullest part)

PERSONAL NOTES
ENERGY LEVEL (circle one)
1 being "I'm so tired I can't get out of bed" and **10 being** "I could dance all night!"

1	2	3	4	5	6	7	8	9	10

SELF ESTEEM/SELF-CONFIDENCE (circle one)
1 being "I can't do anything right" and 10 being **"I'm rea**dy to change the world!"

1	2	3	4	5	6	7	8	9	10

WEEK 13
YOUR WORKOUT AT-A-GLANCE

DAY	WORKOUTS	DURATION
1		min total
2		min total
3		min total
4		min total
5		min total
6		min total
7	Rest	

||||||||||||||||||||||||||||||||||||||||||||||||||||||||||||||||||||||||||||||||||||||||||||||||||||||||

WHAT YOU'LL DO THIS WEEK

- _____
- _____
- _____
- _____
- _____

||||||||||||||||||||||||||||||||||||||||||||||||||||||||||||||||||||||||||||||||||||||||||||||||||||||||

THE WOW FACTOR: Watch Weekend Portions

Even dieters on calorie-controlled plans average an extra 420 calories on weekends, finds a Washington University School of Medicine study—that's enough to stall weight loss. Be a weekend calorie warrior by using smaller plates; carrying healthy, portable snacks such as raw veggies on the go at the mall and steering clear of the food court.

Racette, S. "Influence of Weekend Lifestyle Patterns on Body Weight." *Obesity* (2008), 16(8): 1826-1830

WORKOUT LOG

WORKOUTS	TIME	DURATION
	DAILY TOTAL EXERCISE TIME	

WORKOUT NOTES

How did you feel before? _____

_____

How did you feel after? _____

_____

Any obstacles? _____

_____

Major accomplishment? _____

_____

Other notes: _____

_____

PERSONAL NOTES

ENERGY LEVEL (circle one)
1 being "I'm so tired I can't get out of bed" and **10 being** "I could dance all night!"

1	2	3	4	5	6	7	8	9	10

SELF ESTEEM/SELF-CONFIDENCE (circle one)
1 being "I can't do anything right" and **10 being** "I'm ready to change the world!"

1	2	3	4	5	6	7	8	9	10

FOOD LOG

	FOOD/DRINKS	TIME	CALORIES
Breakfast			
Lunch			
Snack			
Dinner			
Optional Snack			
	DAILY CALORIE TOTAL		

DAILY NUTRITION GOALS:	Grains/Starches	Fruits	Vegetables	Dairy	Healthy Fats	Lean Proteins
	☐☐☐☐☐☐	☐☐☐	☐☐☐☐☐	☐☐☐	☐☐☐☐	☐☐☐
	Water	**Green Tea**	*Optional* (amount per day)			
	☐☐☐☐☐	☐☐☐	Fiber ____ g Calcium ____ mg Vitamin D ____ IU			

BONUS TRACKER (*Record your blood sugar, track your medications, gauge your hunger, or make other notes here.*)

_____

_____

_____

_____

WORKOUT LOG

WORKOUTS	TIME	DURATION
	DAILY TOTAL EXERCISE TIME	

WORKOUT NOTES

How did you feel before? _____

_____

How did you feel after? _____

_____

Any obstacles? _____

_____

Major accomplishment? _____

_____

Other notes: _____

_____

PERSONAL NOTES

ENERGY LEVEL (circle one)
1 being "I'm so tired I can't get out of bed" and **10 being** "I could dance all night!"

1	2	3	4	5	6	7	8	9	10

SELF ESTEEM/SELF-CONFIDENCE (circle one)
1 being "I can't do anything right" and **10 being** "I'm ready to change the world!"

1	2	3	4	5	6	7	8	9	10

FOOD LOG

	FOOD/DRINKS	TIME	CALORIES
Breakfast			
Lunch			
Snack			
Dinner			
Optional Snack			
		DAILY CALORIE TOTAL	

DAILY NUTRITION GOALS:	Grains/Starches ☐☐☐☐☐☐	Fruits ☐☐☐	Vegetables ☐☐☐☐☐	Dairy ☐☐☐	Healthy Fats ☐☐☐☐	Lean Proteins ☐☐☐
	Water ☐☐☐☐☐	Green Tea ☐☐☐	*Optional* (amount per day) Fiber _____ g	Calcium _____ mg		Vitamin D _____ IU

BONUS TRACKER *(Record your blood sugar, track your medications, gauge your hunger, or make other notes here.)*

_____

_____

_____

_____

WORKOUT LOG

WORKOUTS	TIME	DURATION
	DAILY TOTAL EXERCISE TIME	

WORKOUT NOTES

How did you feel before? _____

_____

How did you feel after? _____

_____

Any obstacles? _____

_____

Major accomplishment? _____

_____

Other notes: _____

_____

PERSONAL NOTES

ENERGY LEVEL (circle one)
1 being "I'm so tired I can't get out of bed" and **10 being** "I could dance all night!"

1	2	3	4	5	6	7	8	9	10

SELF ESTEEM/SELF-CONFIDENCE (circle one)
1 being "I can't do anything right" and **10 being** "I'm ready to change the world!"

1	2	3	4	5	6	7	8	9	10

FOOD LOG

	FOOD/DRINKS	TIME	CALORIES
Breakfast			
Lunch			
Snack			
Dinner			
Optional Snack			
	DAILY CALORIE TOTAL		

DAILY NUTRITION GOALS:	Grains/Starches	Fruits	Vegetables	Dairy	Healthy Fats	Lean Proteins
	☐☐☐☐☐☐	☐☐☐	☐☐☐☐☐	☐☐☐	☐☐☐☐	☐☐☐
	Water	Green Tea	Optional (amount per day)			
	☐☐☐☐☐	☐☐☐	Fiber _____ g Calcium _____ mg Vitamin D _____ IU			

BONUS TRACKER (*Record your blood sugar, track your medications, gauge your hunger, or make other notes here.*)

_____

_____

_____

_____

WORKOUT LOG

WORKOUTS	TIME	DURATION
	DAILY TOTAL EXERCISE TIME	

WORKOUT NOTES

How did you feel before? _____

_____

How did you feel after? _____

_____

Any obstacles? _____

_____

Major accomplishment? _____

_____

Other notes: _____

_____

PERSONAL NOTES

ENERGY LEVEL (circle one)
1 being "I'm so tired I can't get out of bed" and **10 being** "I could dance all night!"

1	2	3	4	5	6	7	8	9	10

SELF ESTEEM/SELF-CONFIDENCE (circle one)
1 being "I can't do anything right" and **10 being** "I'm ready to change the world!"

1	2	3	4	5	6	7	8	9	10

FOOD LOG

	FOOD/DRINKS	TIME	CALORIES
Breakfast			
Lunch			
Snack			
Dinner			
Optional Snack			
		DAILY CALORIE TOTAL	

DAILY NUTRITION GOALS:	Grains/Starches ☐☐☐☐☐☐	Fruits ☐☐☐	Vegetables ☐☐☐☐☐	Dairy ☐☐☐	Healthy Fats ☐☐☐☐	Lean Proteins ☐☐☐
	Water ☐☐☐☐☐	**Green Tea** ☐☐☐	*Optional* (amount per day) Fiber _____ g	Calcium _____ mg	Vitamin D _____ IU	

BONUS TRACKER *(Record your blood sugar, track your medications, gauge your hunger, or make other notes here.)*

_____

_____

_____

_____

WORKOUT LOG

WORKOUTS	TIME	DURATION
	DAILY TOTAL EXERCISE TIME	

WORKOUT NOTES

How did you feel before? _____

_____

How did you feel after? _____

_____

Any obstacles? _____

_____

Major accomplishment? _____

_____

Other notes: _____

_____

PERSONAL NOTES

ENERGY LEVEL (circle one)
1 being "I'm so tired I can't get out of bed" and **10 being** "I could dance all night!"

1	2	3	4	5	6	7	8	9	10

SELF ESTEEM/SELF-CONFIDENCE (circle one)
1 being "I can't do anything right" and **10 being** "I'm ready to change the world!"

1	2	3	4	5	6	7	8	9	10

FOOD LOG

	FOOD/DRINKS	TIME	CALORIES
Breakfast			
Lunch			
Snack			
Dinner			
Optional Snack			
	DAILY CALORIE TOTAL		

DAILY NUTRITION GOALS:

Grains/Starches	Fruits	Vegetables	Dairy	Healthy Fats	Lean Proteins
☐☐☐☐☐☐	☐☐☐	☐☐☐☐☐	☐☐☐	☐☐☐☐	☐☐☐

Water	Green Tea	Optional (amount per day)
☐☐☐☐☐	☐☐☐	Fiber _____ g Calcium _____ mg Vitamin D _____ IU

BONUS TRACKER (Record your blood sugar, track your medications, gauge your hunger, or make other notes here.)

_____

_____

_____

_____

WORKOUT LOG

WORKOUTS	TIME	DURATION
	DAILY TOTAL EXERCISE TIME	

WORKOUT NOTES

How did you feel before? _____

_____

How did you feel after? _____

_____

Any obstacles? _____

_____

Major accomplishment? _____

_____

Other notes: _____

_____

PERSONAL NOTES

ENERGY LEVEL (circle one)
1 being "I'm so tired I can't get out of bed" and **10 being** "I could dance all night!"

1	2	3	4	5	6	7	8	9	10

SELF ESTEEM/SELF-CONFIDENCE (circle one)
1 being "I can't do anything right" and **10 being** "I'm ready to change the world!"

1	2	3	4	5	6	7	8	9	10

FOOD LOG

	FOOD/DRINKS	TIME	CALORIES
Breakfast			
Lunch			
Snack			
Dinner			
Optional Snack			
		DAILY CALORIE TOTAL	

DAILY NUTRITION GOALS:	Grains/Starches ☐☐☐☐☐☐	Fruits ☐☐☐	Vegetables ☐☐☐☐☐	Dairy ☐☐☐	Healthy Fats ☐☐☐☐	Lean Proteins ☐☐☐
	Water ☐☐☐☐☐	Green Tea ☐☐☐	Optional (amount per day) Fiber _____ g Calcium _____ mg Vitamin D _____ IU			

BONUS TRACKER (Record your blood sugar, track your medications, gauge your hunger, or make other notes here.)

_____

_____

_____

_____

237

WORKOUT LOG

WORKOUTS	TIME	DURATION
	DAILY TOTAL EXERCISE TIME	

WORKOUT NOTES

How did you feel before? _____

_____

How did you feel after? _____

_____

Any obstacles? _____

_____

Major accomplishment? _____

_____

Other notes: _____

_____

PERSONAL NOTES

ENERGY LEVEL (circle one)
1 being "I'm so tired I can't get out of bed" and **10 being** "I could dance all night!"

1	2	3	4	5	6	7	8	9	10

SELF ESTEEM/SELF-CONFIDENCE (circle one)
1 being "I can't do anything right" and **10 being** "I'm ready to change the world!"

1	2	3	4	5	6	7	8	9	10

FOOD LOG

	FOOD/DRINKS	TIME	CALORIES
Breakfast			
Lunch			
Snack			
Dinner			
Optional Snack			
	DAILY CALORIE TOTAL		

DAILY NUTRITION GOALS:	Grains/Starches ☐☐☐☐☐☐	Fruits ☐☐☐	Vegetables ☐☐☐☐☐	Dairy ☐☐☐	Healthy Fats ☐☐☐☐	Lean Proteins ☐☐☐
	Water ☐☐☐☐☐	Green Tea ☐☐☐	Optional (amount per day) Fiber _____g Calcium _____mg Vitamin D _____IU			

BONUS TRACKER (Record your blood sugar, track your medications, gauge your hunger, or make other notes here.)

_____

_____

_____

_____

239

WEEKLY MEASUREMENTS LOG

WEIGHT _____
LBS

INCHES _____   _____   _____
CHEST   LEFT THIGH   RIGHT THIGH

_____   _____   _____
WAIST   LEFT BICEPS   RIGHT BICEPS

_____
HIPS (at fullest part)

PERSONAL NOTES

ENERGY LEVEL (circle one)
1 being "I'm so tired I can't get out of bed" and **10 being** "I could dance all night!"

1	2	3	4	5	6	7	8	9	10

SELF ESTEEM/SELF-CONFIDENCE (circle one)
1 being "I can't do anything right" and 10 being "**I'm read**y to change the world!"

1	2	3	4	5	6	7	8	9	10

WEEK 14
YOUR WORKOUT AT-A-GLANCE

DAY	WORKOUTS	DURATION
1		min total
2		min total
3		min total
4		min total
5		min total
6		min total
7	Rest	

||||||||||||||||||||||||||||||||||||||||||||||||||||||||||||||||||||||||||||||||||||||||||||||||||||||||||||||

WHAT YOU'LL DO THIS WEEK

- _____
- _____
- _____
- _____
- _____

||||||||||||||||||||||||||||||||||||||||||||||||||||||||||||||||||||||||||||||||||||||||||||||||||||||||||||||

THE WOW FACTOR: Take a Workout Break

A study from England's University of Bristol has uncovered four new reasons to keep workout clothes in your cubicle: On days people fit in exercise before work or over lunch, 79% reported improved mental performance; 74% said they managed their workloads better; 21% reported higher concentration and productivity levels; and 25% made it through the day without unscheduled breaks.

Coulson J, Mckenna J. & Field M. "Exercise at work and work performance." International Journal of Workplace Health Management (2008), 1: 176-197

WORKOUT LOG

WORKOUTS	TIME	DURATION
	DAILY TOTAL EXERCISE TIME	

WORKOUT NOTES

How did you feel before? _____

_____

How did you feel after? _____

_____

Any obstacles? _____

_____

Major accomplishment? _____

_____

Other notes: _____

_____

PERSONAL NOTES

ENERGY LEVEL (circle one)
1 being "I'm so tired I can't get out of bed" and **10 being** "I could dance all night!"

1	2	3	4	5	6	7	8	9	10

SELF ESTEEM/SELF-CONFIDENCE (circle one)
1 being "I can't do anything right" and **10 being** "I'm ready to change the world!"

1	2	3	4	5	6	7	8	9	10

FOOD LOG

	FOOD/DRINKS	TIME	CALORIES
Breakfast			
Lunch			
Snack			
Dinner			
Optional Snack			
	DAILY CALORIE TOTAL		

DAILY NUTRITION GOALS:	Grains/Starches ☐☐☐☐☐☐	Fruits ☐☐☐	Vegetables ☐☐☐☐☐	Dairy ☐☐☐	Healthy Fats ☐☐☐☐	Lean Proteins ☐☐☐
	Water ☐☐☐☐☐	Green Tea ☐☐☐	*Optional* (amount per day) Fiber _____ g Calcium _____ mg **Vitamin D** _____ IU			

BONUS TRACKER *(Record your blood sugar, track your medications, gauge your hunger, or make other notes here.)*

_____

_____

_____

_____

WORKOUT LOG

WORKOUTS	TIME	DURATION
	DAILY TOTAL EXERCISE TIME	

WORKOUT NOTES

How did you feel before? _____

_____

How did you feel after? _____

_____

Any obstacles? _____

_____

Major accomplishment? _____

_____

Other notes: _____

_____

PERSONAL NOTES

ENERGY LEVEL (circle one)
1 being "I'm so tired I can't get out of bed" and **10 being** "I could dance all night!"

1	2	3	4	5	6	7	8	9	10

SELF ESTEEM/SELF-CONFIDENCE (circle one)
1 being "I can't do anything right" and **10 being** "I'm ready to change the world!"

1	2	3	4	5	6	7	8	9	10

FOOD LOG

	FOOD/DRINKS	TIME	CALORIES
Breakfast			
Lunch			
Snack			
Dinner			
Optional Snack			
		DAILY CALORIE TOTAL	

DAILY NUTRITION GOALS:	Grains/Starches ☐☐☐☐☐☐	Fruits ☐☐☐	Vegetables ☐☐☐☐☐	Dairy ☐☐☐	Healthy Fats ☐☐☐☐	Lean Proteins ☐☐☐
	Water ☐☐☐☐☐	Green Tea ☐☐☐	Optional (amount per day) Fiber _____ g Calcium _____ mg Vitamin D _____ IU			

BONUS TRACKER (*Record your blood sugar, track your medications, gauge your hunger, or make other notes here.*)

_____

_____

_____

_____

WORKOUT LOG

WORKOUTS	TIME	DURATION
	DAILY TOTAL EXERCISE TIME	

WORKOUT NOTES

How did you feel before? _____

_____

How did you feel after? _____

_____

Any obstacles? _____

_____

Major accomplishment? _____

_____

Other notes: _____

_____

PERSONAL NOTES

ENERGY LEVEL (circle one)
1 being "I'm so tired I can't get out of bed" and **10 being** "I could dance all night!"

1	2	3	4	5	6	7	8	9	10

SELF ESTEEM/SELF-CONFIDENCE (circle one)
1 being "I can't do anything right" and **10 being** "I'm ready to change the world!"

1	2	3	4	5	6	7	8	9	10

FOOD LOG

	FOOD/DRINKS	TIME	CALORIES
Breakfast			
Lunch			
Snack			
Dinner			
Optional Snack			
		DAILY CALORIE TOTAL	

DAILY NUTRITION GOALS:	Grains/Starches	Fruits	Vegetables	Dairy	Healthy Fats	Lean Proteins
	☐☐☐☐☐☐	☐☐☐	☐☐☐☐☐	☐☐☐	☐☐☐☐	☐☐☐
	Water	Green Tea	Optional (amount per day)			
	☐☐☐☐☐	☐☐☐	Fiber _____ g Calcium _____ mg **Vitamin D** _____ IU			

BONUS TRACKER *(Record your blood sugar, track your medications, gauge your hunger, or make other notes here.)*

_____

_____

_____

_____

247

WORKOUT LOG

WORKOUTS	TIME	DURATION
	DAILY TOTAL EXERCISE TIME	

WORKOUT NOTES

How did you feel before? _____

_____

How did you feel after? _____

_____

Any obstacles? _____

_____

Major accomplishment? _____

_____

Other notes: _____

_____

PERSONAL NOTES

ENERGY LEVEL (circle one)
1 being "I'm so tired I can't get out of bed" and **10 being** "I could dance all night!"

1	2	3	4	5	6	7	8	9	10

SELF ESTEEM/SELF-CONFIDENCE (circle one)
1 being "I can't do anything right" and **10 being** "I'm ready to change the world!"

1	2	3	4	5	6	7	8	9	10

FOOD LOG

	FOOD/DRINKS	TIME	CALORIES
Breakfast			
Lunch			
Snack			
Dinner			
Optional Snack			
		DAILY CALORIE TOTAL	

DAILY NUTRITION GOALS:	Grains/Starches	Fruits	Vegetables	Dairy	Healthy Fats	Lean Proteins
	☐☐☐☐☐☐	☐☐☐	☐☐☐☐☐	☐☐☐	☐☐☐☐	☐☐☐
	Water	Green Tea	Optional (amount per day)			
	☐☐☐☐☐	☐☐☐	Fiber _____ g Calcium _____ mg Vitamin D _____ IU			

BONUS TRACKER *(Record your blood sugar, track your medications, gauge your hunger, or make other notes here.)*

_____

_____

_____

_____

WORKOUT LOG

WORKOUTS	TIME	DURATION
	DAILY TOTAL EXERCISE TIME	

WORKOUT NOTES

How did you feel before? _____

_____

How did you feel after? _____

_____

Any obstacles? _____

_____

Major accomplishment? _____

_____

Other notes: _____

_____

PERSONAL NOTES

ENERGY LEVEL (circle one)
1 being "I'm so tired I can't get out of bed" and **10 being** "I could dance all night!"

1	2	3	4	5	6	7	8	9	10

SELF ESTEEM/SELF-CONFIDENCE (circle one)
1 being "I can't do anything right" and **10 being** "I'm ready to change the world!"

1	2	3	4	5	6	7	8	9	10

FOOD LOG

	FOOD/DRINKS	TIME	CALORIES
Breakfast			
Lunch			
Snack			
Dinner			
Optional Snack			
	DAILY CALORIE TOTAL		

DAILY NUTRITION GOALS:

Grains/Starches	Fruits	Vegetables	Dairy	Healthy Fats	Lean Proteins
☐☐☐☐☐☐	☐☐☐	☐☐☐☐☐	☐☐☐	☐☐☐☐	☐☐☐

Water ☐☐☐☐☐ Green Tea ☐☐☐ *Optional* (amount per day)

Fiber _____ g Calcium _____ mg Vitamin D _____ IU

BONUS TRACKER (*Record your blood sugar, track your medications, gauge your hunger, or make other notes here.*)

_____
_____
_____
_____

251

WORKOUT LOG

WORKOUTS	TIME	DURATION
	DAILY TOTAL EXERCISE TIME	

WORKOUT NOTES

How did you feel before? _____

_____

How did you feel after? _____

_____

Any obstacles? _____

_____

Major accomplishment? _____

_____

Other notes: _____

_____

PERSONAL NOTES

ENERGY LEVEL (circle one)
1 being "I'm so tired I can't get out of bed" and **10 being** "I could dance all night!"

1	2	3	4	5	6	7	8	9	10

SELF ESTEEM/SELF-CONFIDENCE (circle one)
1 being "I can't do anything right" and **10 being** "I'm ready to change the world!"

1	2	3	4	5	6	7	8	9	10

FOOD LOG

	FOOD/DRINKS	TIME	CALORIES
Breakfast			
Lunch			
Snack			
Dinner			
Optional Snack			
		DAILY CALORIE TOTAL	

DAILY NUTRITION GOALS:	Grains/Starches	Fruits	Vegetables	Dairy	Healthy Fats	Lean Proteins
	☐☐☐☐☐☐	☐☐☐	☐☐☐☐☐	☐☐☐	☐☐☐☐	☐☐☐
	Water	Green Tea	Optional (amount per day)			
	☐☐☐☐☐	☐☐☐	Fiber _____ g Calcium _____ mg Vitamin D _____ IU			

BONUS TRACKER *(Record your blood sugar, track your medications, gauge your hunger, or make other notes here.)*

_____

_____

_____

_____

253

WORKOUT LOG

WORKOUTS	TIME	DURATION
	DAILY TOTAL EXERCISE TIME	

WORKOUT NOTES

How did you feel before? _____

_____

How did you feel after? _____

_____

Any obstacles? _____

_____

Major accomplishment? _____

_____

Other notes: _____

_____

PERSONAL NOTES

ENERGY LEVEL (circle one)
1 being "I'm so tired I can't get out of bed" and **10 being** "I could dance all night!"

1	2	3	4	5	6	7	8	9	10

SELF ESTEEM/SELF-CONFIDENCE (circle one)
1 being "I can't do anything right" and **10 being** "I'm ready to change the world!"

1	2	3	4	5	6	7	8	9	10

FOOD LOG

	FOOD/DRINKS	TIME	CALORIES
Breakfast			
Lunch			
Snack			
Dinner			
Optional Snack			
		DAILY CALORIE TOTAL	

DAILY NUTRITION GOALS:	Grains/Starches ☐☐☐☐☐☐	Fruits ☐☐☐	Vegetables ☐☐☐☐☐	Dairy ☐☐☐	Healthy Fats ☐☐☐☐	Lean Proteins ☐☐☐
	Water ☐☐☐☐☐	Green Tea ☐☐☐	*Optional* (amount per day) Fiber _____ g Calcium _____ mg Vitamin D _____ IU			

BONUS TRACKER *(Record your blood sugar, track your medications, gauge your hunger, or make other notes here.)*

_____

_____

_____

_____

WEEKLY MEASUREMENTS LOG

WEIGHT　_____
LBS

INCHES　_____　　_____　　_____
　　　　　CHEST　　　LEFT THIGH　　RIGHT THIGH

　　　　　_____　　_____　　_____
　　　　　WAIST　　　LEFT BICEPS　　RIGHT BICEPS

　　　　　_____
　　　　　HIPS (at fullest part)

PERSONAL NOTES

ENERGY LEVEL (circle one)
1 being "I'm so tired I can't get out of bed" and **10 being** "I could dance all night!"

1	2	3	4	5	6	7	8	9	10

SELF ESTEEM/SELF-CONFIDENCE (circle one)
1 being "I can't do anything right" and 10 being **"I'm rea**dy to change the world!"

1	2	3	4	5	6	7	8	9	10

WEEK 15
YOUR WORKOUT AT-A-GLANCE

DAY	WORKOUTS	DURATION
1		min total
2		min total
3		min total
4		min total
5		min total
6		min total
7	Rest	

WHAT YOU'LL DO THIS WEEK

- _____
- _____
- _____
- _____
- _____

THE WOW FACTOR: De-stress While You Stretch

You may rely on your workout to help you relax, but exercisers who started their strength-training routines without any feelings of stress improved their strength 25% more than the stressed group, according to a University of Texas study. To unwind before you exercise, try a relaxing warm-up followed by some soothing stretches and gentle yoga poses.

Bartholomew, J., StultsS-Kolehmainen, M., Elrod, C., and Todd, J. "Stength Gains After Resistance Training: The effect of stressful, negative life events." *Journal of Strength and Conditioning Research* (2008), 22(4):1215-1221

WORKOUT LOG

WORKOUTS	TIME	DURATION
	DAILY TOTAL EXERCISE TIME	

WORKOUT NOTES

How did you feel before? _____

_____

How did you feel after? _____

_____

Any obstacles? _____

_____

Major accomplishment? _____

_____

Other notes: _____

_____

PERSONAL NOTES

ENERGY LEVEL (circle one)
1 being "I'm so tired I can't get out of bed" and **10 being** "I could dance all night!"

1	2	3	4	5	6	7	8	9	10

SELF-ESTEEM/SELF-CONFIDENCE (circle one)
1 being "I can't do anything right" and **10 being** "I'm ready to change the world!"

1	2	3	4	5	6	7	8	9	10

FOOD LOG

	FOOD/DRINKS	TIME	CALORIES
Breakfast			
Lunch			
Snack			
Dinner			
Optional Snack			
		DAILY CALORIE TOTAL	

DAILY NUTRITION GOALS:	Grains/Starches ☐☐☐☐☐☐	Fruits ☐☐☐	Vegetables ☐☐☐☐☐	Dairy ☐☐☐	Healthy Fats ☐☐☐☐	Lean Proteins ☐☐☐
	Water ☐☐☐☐☐	Green Tea ☐☐☐	*Optional* (amount per day) Fiber _____ g **Calcium** _____ mg **Vitamin D** _____ IU			

BONUS TRACKER *(Record your blood sugar, track your medications, gauge your hunger, or make other notes here.)*

_____

_____

_____

_____

WORKOUT LOG

WORKOUTS	TIME	DURATION
	DAILY TOTAL EXERCISE TIME	

WORKOUT NOTES

How did you feel before? _____

_____

How did you feel after? _____

_____

Any obstacles? _____

_____

Major accomplishment? _____

_____

Other notes: _____

_____

PERSONAL NOTES

ENERGY LEVEL (circle one)
1 being "I'm so tired I can't get out of bed" and **10 being** "I could dance all night!"

1	2	3	4	5	6	7	8	9	10

SELF-ESTEEM/SELF-CONFIDENCE (circle one)
1 being "I can't do anything right" and **10 being** "I'm ready to change the world!"

1	2	3	4	5	6	7	8	9	10

FOOD LOG

	FOOD/DRINKS	TIME	CALORIES
Breakfast			
Lunch			
Snack			
Dinner			
Optional Snack			
		DAILY CALORIE TOTAL	

DAILY NUTRITION GOALS:	Grains/Starches ☐☐☐☐☐☐	Fruits ☐☐☐	Vegetables ☐☐☐☐☐	Dairy ☐☐☐	Healthy Fats ☐☐☐☐	Lean Proteins ☐☐☐
	Water ☐☐☐☐☐	Green Tea ☐☐☐	Optional (amount per day) Fiber _____ g Calcium _____ mg Vitamin D _____ IU			

BONUS TRACKER (*Record your blood sugar, track your medications, gauge your hunger, or make other notes here.*)

_____

_____

_____

_____

WORKOUT LOG

WORKOUTS	TIME	DURATION
	DAILY TOTAL EXERCISE TIME	

WORKOUT NOTES

How did you feel before? _____

_____

How did you feel after? _____

_____

Any obstacles? _____

_____

Major accomplishment? _____

_____

Other notes: _____

_____

PERSONAL NOTES

ENERGY LEVEL (circle one)
1 being "I'm so tired I can't get out of bed" and **10 being** "I could dance all night!"

1	2	3	4	5	6	7	8	9	10

SELF-ESTEEM/SELF-CONFIDENCE (circle one)
1 being "I can't do anything right" and **10 being** "I'm ready to change the world!"

1	2	3	4	5	6	7	8	9	10

FOOD LOG

	FOOD/DRINKS	TIME	CALORIES
Breakfast			
Lunch			
Snack			
Dinner			
Optional Snack			
	DAILY CALORIE TOTAL		

DAILY NUTRITION GOALS:	Grains/Starches	Fruits	Vegetables	Dairy	Healthy Fats	Lean Proteins
	☐☐☐☐☐☐	☐☐☐	☐☐☐☐☐	☐☐☐	☐☐☐☐	☐☐☐
	Water	**Green Tea**	*Optional* (amount per day)			
	☐☐☐☐☐	☐☐☐	**Fiber** _____ g **Calcium** _____ mg **Vitamin D** _____ IU			

BONUS TRACKER *(Record your blood sugar, track your medications, gauge your hunger, or make other notes here.)*

_____

_____

_____

_____

WORKOUT LOG

WORKOUTS	TIME	DURATION
	DAILY TOTAL EXERCISE TIME	

WORKOUT NOTES

How did you feel before? _____

_____

How did you feel after? _____

_____

Any obstacles? _____

_____

Major accomplishment? _____

_____

Other notes: _____

_____

PERSONAL NOTES

ENERGY LEVEL (circle one)
1 being "I'm so tired I can't get out of bed" and **10 being** "I could dance all night!"

1	2	3	4	5	6	7	8	9	10

SELF-ESTEEM/SELF-CONFIDENCE (circle one)
1 being "I can't do anything right" and **10 being** "I'm ready to change the world!"

1	2	3	4	5	6	7	8	9	10

FOOD LOG

	FOOD/DRINKS	TIME	CALORIES
Breakfast			
Lunch			
Snack			
Dinner			
Optional Snack			
	DAILY CALORIE TOTAL		

DAILY NUTRITION GOALS:	Grains/Starches	Fruits	Vegetables	Dairy	Healthy Fats	Lean Proteins
	☐☐☐☐☐☐	☐☐☐	☐☐☐☐☐	☐☐☐	☐☐☐☐	☐☐☐
	Water	Green Tea	Optional (amount per day)			
	☐☐☐☐☐	☐☐☐	Fiber _____ g Calcium _____ mg Vitamin D _____ IU			

BONUS TRACKER *(Record your blood sugar, track your medications, gauge your hunger, or make other notes here.)*

_____

_____

_____

_____

WORKOUT LOG

WORKOUTS	TIME	DURATION
	DAILY TOTAL EXERCISE TIME	

WORKOUT NOTES

How did you feel before? _____

_____

How did you feel after? _____

_____

Any obstacles? _____

_____

Major accomplishment? _____

_____

Other notes: _____

_____

PERSONAL NOTES

ENERGY LEVEL (circle one)
1 being "I'm so tired I can't get out of bed" and **10 being** "I could dance all night!"

1	2	3	4	5	6	7	8	9	10

SELF-ESTEEM/SELF-CONFIDENCE (circle one)
1 being "I can't do anything right" and **10 being** "I'm ready to change the world!"

1	2	3	4	5	6	7	8	9	10

FOOD LOG

	FOOD/DRINKS	TIME	CALORIES
Breakfast			
Lunch			
Snack			
Dinner			
Optional Snack			
	DAILY CALORIE TOTAL		

DAILY NUTRITION GOALS:	Grains/Starches	Fruits	Vegetables	Dairy	Healthy Fats	Lean Proteins
	☐☐☐☐☐☐	☐☐☐	☐☐☐☐☐	☐☐☐	☐☐☐☐	☐☐☐
	Water	Green Tea	*Optional* (amount per day)			
	☐☐☐☐☐	☐☐☐	Fiber _____ g Calcium _____ mg **Vitamin D** _____ IU			

BONUS TRACKER *(Record your blood sugar, track your medications, gauge your hunger, or make other notes here.)*

_____

_____

_____

_____

WORKOUT LOG

WORKOUTS	TIME	DURATION
	DAILY TOTAL EXERCISE TIME	

WORKOUT NOTES

How did you feel before? _____

_____

How did you feel after? _____

_____

Any obstacles? _____

_____

Major accomplishment? _____

_____

Other notes: _____

_____

PERSONAL NOTES

ENERGY LEVEL (circle one)
1 being "I'm so tired I can't get out of bed" and **10 being** "I could dance all night!"

1	2	3	4	5	6	7	8	9	10

SELF-ESTEEM/SELF-CONFIDENCE (circle one)
1 being "I can't do anything right" and **10 being** "I'm ready to change the world!"

1	2	3	4	5	6	7	8	9	10

FOOD LOG

	FOOD/DRINKS	TIME	CALORIES
Breakfast			
Lunch			
Snack			
Dinner			
Optional Snack			
		DAILY CALORIE TOTAL	

DAILY NUTRITION GOALS:	Grains/Starches	Fruits	Vegetables	Dairy	Healthy Fats	Lean Proteins
	☐☐☐☐☐☐	☐☐☐	☐☐☐☐☐	☐☐☐	☐☐☐☐	☐☐☐
	Water	Green Tea	Optional (amount per day)			
	☐☐☐☐☐	☐☐☐	Fiber ____g Calcium ____mg Vitamin D ____IU			

BONUS TRACKER (Record your blood sugar, track your medications, gauge your hunger, or make other notes here.)

_____

_____

_____

_____

WORKOUT LOG

WORKOUTS	TIME	DURATION
	DAILY TOTAL EXERCISE TIME	

WORKOUT NOTES

How did you feel before? _____

_____

How did you feel after? _____

_____

Any obstacles? _____

_____

Major accomplishment? _____

_____

Other notes: _____

_____

PERSONAL NOTES

ENERGY LEVEL (circle one)
1 being "I'm so tired I can't get out of bed" and **10 being** "I could dance all night!"

1	2	3	4	5	6	7	8	9	10

SELF-ESTEEM/SELF-CONFIDENCE (circle one)
1 being "I can't do anything right" and **10 being** "I'm ready to change the world!"

1	2	3	4	5	6	7	8	9	10

FOOD LOG

	FOOD/DRINKS	TIME	CALORIES
Breakfast			
Lunch			
Snack			
Dinner			
Optional Snack			
	DAILY CALORIE TOTAL		

DAILY NUTRITION GOALS:	Grains/Starches ☐☐☐☐☐☐	Fruits ☐☐☐	Vegetables ☐☐☐☐☐	Dairy ☐☐☐	Healthy Fats ☐☐☐☐	Lean Proteins ☐☐☐
	Water ☐☐☐☐☐	Green Tea ☐☐☐	*Optional* (amount per day) Fiber _____ g **Calcium** _____ mg **Vitamin D** _____ IU			

BONUS TRACKER *(Record your blood sugar, track your medications, gauge your hunger, or make other notes here.)*

_____

_____

_____

_____

WEEKLY MEASUREMENTS LOG

WEIGHT　　_____
　　　　　　LBS

INCHES　　_____　　_____　　_____
　　　　　　CHEST　　　LEFT THIGH　　RIGHT THIGH

　　　　　　_____　　_____　　_____
　　　　　　WAIST　　　LEFT BICEPS　　RIGHT BICEPS

　　　　　　_____
　　　　　　HIPS (at fullest part)

PERSONAL NOTES

ENERGY LEVEL (circle one)
1 being "I'm so tired I can't get out of bed" and **10 being** "I could dance all night!"

1	2	3	4	5	6	7	8	9	10

SELF-ESTEEM/SELF-CONFIDENCE (circle one)
1 being "I can't do anything right" and **10 being** "I'm ready to change the world!"

1	2	3	4	5	6	7	8	9	10

WEEK 16
YOUR WORKOUT AT-A-GLANCE

DAY	WORKOUTS	DURATION
1		min total
2		min total
3		min total
4		min total
5		min total
6		min total
7	Rest	

WHAT YOU'LL DO THIS WEEK

- _____
- _____
- _____
- _____
- _____

THE WOW FACTOR: Ditch Cell Phone Chatting

A study from the University of Illinois shows that pedestrians who walked through virtual streets while talking on a cell phone (even hands-free) were more distracted. They took 25% longer to cross streets, and were as much as 15% more likely to be in an accident than those who walked while listening to music. It's still smart to carry a cell phone in case of an emergency, but if you want to talk, walk with another person.

Neider, M.B., et al., Pedestrians, vehicles, and cell phones. Accid. Anal. Prev. (2009), doi:10.1016/j.aap.2009.10.004

WORKOUT LOG

WORKOUTS	TIME	DURATION
	DAILY TOTAL EXERCISE TIME	

WORKOUT NOTES

How did you feel before? _____

_____

How did you feel after? _____

_____

Any obstacles? _____

_____

Major accomplishment? _____

_____

Other notes: _____

_____

PERSONAL NOTES

ENERGY LEVEL (circle one)
1 being "I'm so tired I can't get out of bed" and **10 being** "I could dance all night!"

1	2	3	4	5	6	7	8	9	10

SELF-ESTEEM/SELF-CONFIDENCE (circle one)
1 being "I can't do anything right" and **10 being** "I'm ready to change the world!"

1	2	3	4	5	6	7	8	9	10

FOOD LOG

	FOOD/DRINKS	TIME	CALORIES
Breakfast			
Lunch			
Snack			
Dinner			
Optional Snack			
	DAILY CALORIE TOTAL		

DAILY NUTRITION GOALS:	**Grains/Starches** ☐☐☐☐☐☐	**Fruits** ☐☐☐	**Vegetables** ☐☐☐☐☐	**Dairy** ☐☐☐	**Healthy Fats** ☐☐☐☐	**Lean Proteins** ☐☐☐
	Water ☐☐☐☐☐	**Green Tea** ☐☐☐	*Optional* (amount per day) Fiber _____g **Calcium** _____mg **Vitamin D** _____IU			

BONUS TRACKER *(Record your blood sugar, track your medications, gauge your hunger, or make other notes here.)*

_____

_____

_____

_____

WORKOUT LOG

WORKOUTS	TIME	DURATION
	DAILY TOTAL EXERCISE TIME	

WORKOUT NOTES

How did you feel before? _____

_____

How did you feel after? _____

_____

Any obstacles? _____

_____

Major accomplishment? _____

_____

Other notes: _____

_____

PERSONAL NOTES

ENERGY LEVEL (circle one)
1 being "I'm so tired I can't get out of bed" and **10 being** "I could dance all night!"

1	2	3	4	5	6	7	8	9	10

SELF-ESTEEM/SELF-CONFIDENCE (circle one)
1 being "I can't do anything right" and **10 being** "I'm ready to change the world!"

1	2	3	4	5	6	7	8	9	10

FOOD LOG

	FOOD/DRINKS	TIME	CALORIES
Breakfast			
Lunch			
Snack			
Dinner			
Optional Snack			
	DAILY CALORIE TOTAL		

DAILY NUTRITION GOALS:	Grains/Starches ☐☐☐☐☐☐	Fruits ☐☐☐	Vegetables ☐☐☐☐☐	Dairy ☐☐☐	Healthy Fats ☐☐☐☐	Lean Proteins ☐☐☐
	Water ☐☐☐☐☐	Green Tea ☐☐☐	Optional (amount per day) Fiber _____ g	Calcium _____ mg	Vitamin D _____ IU	

BONUS TRACKER *(Record your blood sugar, track your medications, gauge your hunger, or make other notes here.)*

_____

_____

_____

_____

WORKOUT LOG

WORKOUTS	TIME	DURATION
	DAILY TOTAL EXERCISE TIME	

WORKOUT NOTES

How did you feel before? _____

_____

How did you feel after? _____

_____

Any obstacles? _____

_____

Major accomplishment? _____

_____

Other notes: _____

_____

PERSONAL NOTES

ENERGY LEVEL (circle one)
1 being "I'm so tired I can't get out of bed" and **10 being** "I could dance all night!"

1	2	3	4	5	6	7	8	9	10

SELF-ESTEEM/SELF-CONFIDENCE (circle one)
1 being "I can't do anything right" and **10 being** "I'm ready to change the world!"

1	2	3	4	5	6	7	8	9	10

FOOD LOG

	FOOD/DRINKS	TIME	CALORIES
Breakfast			
Lunch			
Snack			
Dinner			
Optional Snack			
		DAILY CALORIE TOTAL	

DAILY NUTRITION GOALS:	Grains/Starches ☐☐☐☐☐☐	Fruits ☐☐☐	Vegetables ☐☐☐☐☐	Dairy ☐☐☐	Healthy Fats ☐☐☐☐	Lean Proteins ☐☐☐
	Water ☐☐☐☐☐	Green Tea ☐☐☐	Optional (amount per day) Fiber ___ g Calcium ___ mg Vitamin D ___ IU			

BONUS TRACKER *(Record your blood sugar, track your medications, gauge your hunger, or make other notes here.)*

_____

_____

_____

_____

279

WORKOUT LOG

WORKOUTS	TIME	DURATION
	DAILY TOTAL EXERCISE TIME	

WORKOUT NOTES

How did you feel before? _____

_____

How did you feel after? _____

_____

Any obstacles? _____

_____

Major accomplishment? _____

_____

Other notes: _____

_____

PERSONAL NOTES

ENERGY LEVEL (circle one)
1 being "I'm so tired I can't get out of bed" and **10 being** "I could dance all night!"

1	2	3	4	5	6	7	8	9	10

SELF-ESTEEM/SELF-CONFIDENCE (circle one)
1 being "I can't do anything right" and **10 being** "I'm ready to change the world!"

1	2	3	4	5	6	7	8	9	10

FOOD LOG

	FOOD/DRINKS	TIME	CALORIES
Breakfast			
Lunch			
Snack			
Dinner			
Optional Snack			
		DAILY CALORIE TOTAL	

DAILY NUTRITION GOALS:	Grains/Starches	Fruits	Vegetables	Dairy	Healthy Fats	Lean Proteins
	☐☐☐☐☐☐	☐☐☐	☐☐☐☐☐	☐☐☐	☐☐☐☐	☐☐☐
	Water	Green Tea	Optional (amount per day)			
	☐☐☐☐☐	☐☐☐	Fiber _____ g Calcium _____ mg Vitamin D _____ IU			

BONUS TRACKER (*Record your blood sugar, track your medications, gauge your hunger, or make other notes here.*)

_____

_____

_____

_____

WORKOUT LOG

WORKOUTS	TIME	DURATION
	DAILY TOTAL EXERCISE TIME	

WORKOUT NOTES

How did you feel before? _____

_____

How did you feel after? _____

_____

Any obstacles? _____

_____

Major accomplishment? _____

_____

Other notes: _____

_____

PERSONAL NOTES

ENERGY LEVEL (circle one)
1 being "I'm so tired I can't get out of bed" and **10 being** "I could dance all night!"

1	2	3	4	5	6	7	8	9	10

SELF-ESTEEM/SELF-CONFIDENCE (circle one)
1 being "I can't do anything right" and **10 being** "I'm ready to change the world!"

1	2	3	4	5	6	7	8	9	10

FOOD LOG

	FOOD/DRINKS	TIME	CALORIES
Breakfast			
Lunch			
Snack			
Dinner			
Optional Snack			
	DAILY CALORIE TOTAL		

DAILY NUTRITION GOALS:	Grains/Starches	Fruits	Vegetables	Dairy	Healthy Fats	Lean Proteins
	☐☐☐☐☐☐	☐☐☐	☐☐☐☐☐	☐☐☐	☐☐☐☐	☐☐☐
	Water	Green Tea	Optional (amount per day)			
	☐☐☐☐☐	☐☐☐	Fiber _____ g Calcium _____ mg Vitamin D _____ IU			

BONUS TRACKER *(Record your blood sugar, track your medications, gauge your hunger, or make other notes here.)*

_____

_____

_____

_____

WORKOUT LOG

WORKOUTS	TIME	DURATION
	DAILY TOTAL EXERCISE TIME	

WORKOUT NOTES

How did you feel before? _____

_____

How did you feel after? _____

_____

Any obstacles? _____

_____

Major accomplishment? _____

_____

Other notes: _____

_____

PERSONAL NOTES

ENERGY LEVEL (circle one)
1 being "I'm so tired I can't get out of bed" and **10 being** "I could dance all night!"

1	2	3	4	5	6	7	8	9	10

SELF-ESTEEM/SELF-CONFIDENCE (circle one)
1 being "I can't do anything right" and **10 being** "I'm ready to change the world!"

1	2	3	4	5	6	7	8	9	10

FOOD LOG

	FOOD/DRINKS	TIME	CALORIES
Breakfast			
Lunch			
Snack			
Dinner			
Optional Snack			
	DAILY CALORIE TOTAL		

DAILY NUTRITION GOALS:	Grains/Starches	Fruits	Vegetables	Dairy	Healthy Fats	Lean Proteins
	☐☐☐☐☐☐	☐☐☐	☐☐☐☐☐	☐☐☐	☐☐☐☐	☐☐☐
	Water	**Green Tea**	*Optional* (amount per day)			
	☐☐☐☐☐	☐☐☐	Fiber _____ g Calcium _____ mg Vitamin D _____ IU			

BONUS TRACKER *(Record your blood sugar, track your medications, gauge your hunger, or make other notes here.)*

_____

_____

_____

_____

WORKOUT LOG

WORKOUTS	TIME	DURATION
	DAILY TOTAL EXERCISE TIME	

WORKOUT NOTES

How did you feel before? _____

_____

How did you feel after? _____

_____

Any obstacles? _____

_____

Major accomplishment? _____

_____

Other notes: _____

_____

PERSONAL NOTES

ENERGY LEVEL (circle one)
1 being "I'm so tired I can't get out of bed" and **10 being** "I could dance all night!"

1	2	3	4	5	6	7	8	9	10

SELF-ESTEEM/SELF-CONFIDENCE (circle one)
1 being "I can't do anything right" and **10 being** "I'm ready to change the world!"

1	2	3	4	5	6	7	8	9	10

BEYOND 8 WEEKS **WALK OFF WEIGHT**

FOOD LOG

	FOOD/DRINKS	TIME	CALORIES
Breakfast			
Lunch			
Snack			
Dinner			
Optional Snack			
	DAILY CALORIE TOTAL		

DAILY NUTRITION GOALS:	Grains/Starches	Fruits	Vegetables	Dairy	Healthy Fats	Lean Proteins
	☐☐☐☐☐☐	☐☐☐	☐☐☐☐☐	☐☐☐	☐☐☐☐	☐☐☐
	Water	Green Tea	Optional (amount per day)			
	☐☐☐☐☐	☐☐☐	Fiber ____g Calcium ____mg Vitamin D ____IU			

BONUS TRACKER (*Record your blood sugar, track your medications, gauge your hunger, or make other notes here.*)

_____

_____

_____

_____

WEEKLY MEASUREMENTS LOG

WEIGHT　_____
LBS

INCHES　_____　_____　_____
CHEST　　　　LEFT THIGH　　RIGHT THIGH

_____　_____　_____
WAIST　　　　LEFT BICEPS　RIGHT BICEPS

_____
HIPS (at fullest part)

PERSONAL NOTES

ENERGY LEVEL (circle one)
1 being "I'm so tired I can't get out of bed" and **10 being** "I could dance all night!"

1	2	3	4	5	6	7	8	9	10

SELF-ESTEEM/SELF-CONFIDENCE (circle one)
1 being "I can't do anything right" and **10 being** "I'm ready to change the world!"

1	2	3	4	5	6	7	8	9	10